S. Stepniak

The Russian Storm-Cloud

Or, Russia in her Relations to neighbouring Countries

S. Stepniak

The Russian Storm-Cloud
Or, Russia in her Relations to neighbouring Countries

ISBN/EAN: 9783337168728

Printed in Europe, USA, Canada, Australia, Japan

Cover: Foto ©ninafisch / pixelio.de

More available books at **www.hansebooks.com**

THE RUSSIAN STORM-CLOUD;

OR,

Russia in her Relations to Neighbouring Countries.

BY

STEPNIAK,

AUTHOR OF "RUSSIA UNDER THE TSARS," "UNDERGROUND RUSSIA," ETC.

LONDON:
SWAN SONNENSCHEIN AND CO.
PATERNOSTER SQUARE.

1886.

Printed by Hazell, Watson, & Viney, Ld., London and Aylesbury.

PREFACE.

In this volume, which I have the honour to present to the indulgence of English readers, I deal with the two contending principles of modern Russia—Liberty and Despotism—from one particular point of view, viz., the influence both are likely to exercise upon neighbouring European countries and their general welfare and progress. The entire work is entitled "The Russian Storm-Cloud," under which title the first four chapters appeared in *Time*. Ever since the creation of the Russian Empire by Peter the Great, Europe has felt uneasy, and still feels apprehensive at the vicinity of a colossal State obedient to the despotic will of one man and the continual extension of the empire in all directions. On the other hand, Russian revolution, owing to the extremely violent character of the means adopted, appeared, and still appears, to many minds as a threatening phantom of general destruction and of the overthrow of all social order, scarcely less dangerous to the peace of Europe than to the despotism of the Tzar.

My object has been to indicate the rival nature

and character of both of these elements. The book is, therefore, essentially a political one. But I have done my best to make it as objective as possible,—describing our country, rather than advocating any opinion, exposing facts which might enable the reader to draw his conclusions instead of forcing on him my own.

The article on Poland, together with those on "European Socialism and the Dynamite Epidemic," and "A Revolt or a Revolution?" were written to complete the present volume. The chapters on "The Russian Army" and on "Terrorism in Russia and in Europe," are reprinted, by the kind permission of the publishers, from the *Times* and the *Contemporary Review*, to whom I must once more express my earnest thanks for their uniform courtesy.

CONTENTS.

		PAGE
I. THE RUSSIAN STORM-CLOUD:—		
I. What do the Nihilists want?		1
II. What are the Forces the Russian Revolution commands?		18
III. Why Russia is a Conquering Country		47
IV. The Political Form of the Russia of the Future		83
II. THE RUSSIAN ARMY AND ITS COMMISSARIAT		97
III. YOUNG POLAND AND RUSSIAN REVOLUTION		139
IV. TERRORISM IN RUSSIA AND TERRORISM IN EUROPE		175
V. EUROPEAN SOCIALISM AND THE DYNAMITE EPIDEMIC		207
VI. A REVOLT OR A REVOLUTION?		229

I.

THE RUSSIAN STORM-CLOUD.

CHAPTER I.

WHAT DO THE NIHILISTS WANT?

I.

SHORTLY after the Winter Palace explosion I remember having seen in an English satirical paper the following caricature:—Two Nihilists are meeting amidst heaps of ruins. "Is all blown up already?" asks one of them. "No," answers the other. "The globe remains firm still." "Well, let us blow up the globe then!" exclaims the first.

This was a graphical representation of the general conception about the Nihilists just in the epoch when their name was in everybody's mouth.

Five years followed, bringing with them, among other facts of Nihilist history, some dozen of trials, the most striking of them—that of Tzaricides, for example—having a certain publicity, which enabled the accused to explain before the audience and reporters of foreign papers the real character and aim of the movement. The Nihilists' clandestine publications, hitherto completely ignored, are now noticed by the best papers. The Nihilists' manifestoes are reprinted; clandestine papers are epitomised. We—Nihilists living abroad—did all we could to satisfy the growing desire of the European public to know something about our movement. All this has wrought a notable change in the minds of Europeans. Here, in England there are many who understand that the Nihilists are not at all apostles of destruction, and who, though very moderate in their opinion, agree that under such a *régime* as that of Russia nobody has a right to blame the people when they take the laws into their own hands. " Were I a Russian I should be a Nihilist myself." That is a phrase which I can testify to have very often heard from all classes in England. And out of many expressions of sympathy, I will here quote one as belonging to a paper, by no means a subversive one, the *Christian World*, which, in noticing one of my articles in the *Times*, says :—" Nor is it wonderful that now and again the wrath of the Russian people finds expression in actions which are called crimes, because they happen to-day ; but which, when we read them in the pages of history, we think of as testimonies of the patriotism of people who were incapable of enduring the wrongs which base tyrannies conceived and imposed " (September 11th, 1884).

But in this time of febrile activity, when people hardly notice what they pass by, or, having noticed, forget it at once, new conceptions enter very slowly into the public mind. And to destroy an inveterate prejudice a vast quantity of printer's ink must be wasted. There is no help for it. This philosophy of patience was forced on me—I may be excused for mentioning it—by reading the many notices which honoured my last book, " Russia Under the Tzars." Very careful and often very indulgent on other points, many of the best-informed and most respectable papers have made some really surprising blunders in speaking of the tendencies of the "Nihilists." The impartial *Athenæum*, while very appreciative as to the work itself, and deeply impressed by the horrors of Russian prisons described in it, observes that English readers must not forget that the Nihilists are people who are "resolved to force upon an unprepared, if not an unwilling, country the fantastic freedom of anarchy." The *Morning Post* is still more categorical in its assertion. This respectable paper is quite aware that the Nihilists "do not work for reforms, or for amelioration of popular burdens, but for the destruction of political and social order." The *St. James's Gazette* seems to hold the same opinion: "To the Nihilist's mind nothing short of total destruction of the State seems worth a moment's serious consideration."

The best means to get rid of such misconception would be, perhaps, to abandon the ill-sounding name by which our party is designated. "Nihilism" means "Nothingness." "Nihilists," many people conclude, without much trouble, must then be partisans of general destruction. The thing is clear and simple, and easily remembered. "The very name which the revolutionists have assumed is a sufficient argument against them," says the *Morning Post*. Yes, it would be an argument were it really assumed by them. But every Russian, or student of Russian things, will affirm that it is not so. The Revolutionists call themselves, and are called in their country, by a good many names—"Social-revolutionist" in the "high" style of manifestoes, or more briefly "revolutionist;" and in colloquial slang, which is more usual, simply "radicals." They were baptised with the name "Nihilist" by a whim of European current journalism, which, wanting some name for them, borrowed from Ivan Turgheneff's novel the first that came to hand. However it be, the name is so deeply rooted in popular minds, that it is impossible to change it; at all events, more difficult than to attach to it a sort of glossary.

To cut short all babbling about the Nihilists' thirst for destruction, I will make a brief quotation from a well-known document,—the letter of the Nihilists' Executive Committee to Alexander III., issued after his accession to the throne. I pass over the explanatory part of this manifesto, in which the blood-thirsty Nihilists show how unwilling they are to use the violent means to which the Government has driven them; how anxious they would be to avoid, "in the interest of the country," violent revolutions, "which are an enormous waste of strength and energy, capable of being applied in other conditions to useful works, to the development of popular intelligence, and of general prosperity;" and how eager they are to abstain from taking the law into their own hands. Suffice it to reproduce the few lines in which the Committee point out their conditions for the cessation of hostilities.

"First, a general amnesty for all political offenders, since they have committed no crime, but have simply done their duty as citizens.

"Second, the convocation of the representatives of the whole of the people, for the examination of the best forms of social and political life, according to the wants and desires of the people.

"We, nevertheless, consider it necessary to point out that the legalisation of power by the representation of the people can only be arrived at when the elections are perfectly free. The elections should, therefore, take place under the following conditions :—

"First, the deputies shall be chosen by all classes without distinction, in proportion to the number of inhabitants.

"Second, there shall be no restriction of any kind upon electors or deputies.

"Third, the elections and the electoral agitation shall be perfectly free. The Government will, therefore, grant, as provisional regulations, until the convocation of the popular assemblies :—

"(a) Complete freedom of the press.
"(b) Complete freedom of speech.
"(c) Complete freedom of public meeting.
"(d) Complete freedom of electoral addresses.

"These are the only means by which Russia can enter upon the path of peaceful and regular development. We solemnly declare, before the country, and before the whole world, that our party will submit unconditionally to the National Assembly which meets upon the basis of the above conditions, and will offer no opposition to the Government which the National Assembly may sanction."

This document, issued in many thousand copies for interior circulation, was translated and reprinted in all the leading foreign papers, and made its way through all Europe. It startled European readers as something quite unexpected from such people as the Nihilists; but this was due to the great ignorance prevailing about Russian matters. The letter to Alexander III. said nothing essentially new. Every attempt against Alexander II. after that of Solovieff was followed by a declaration of the Nihilist Committee, that the hostilities against his person would cease immediately, if the Emperor would resign into the hands of a National Representative Assembly (Zemsky Sobor) his autocratic power The letter to Alexander III. gave only more detail and precision to those declarations.

Such desiderata leave little room indeed for accusing the Nihilists of being wild fanatics, striving to "impose on the unprepared nation" some Utopian scheme. Let me point out, though republican by their personal preference, they do not ask even for the abolition of monarchy, but only for the abolition of its exorbitant power, by placing the supreme control over State affairs in the hands of a National Assembly; efforts which surely cannot be identified with the "total destruction of the State," or of "political and social order," since such things have existed in all civilised countries for generations, sometimes for centuries, without producing in the least degree such dreadful consequences.

But is the ideal of the Russian Nihilists limited to a free constitution? No. Not at all. They never winced from declaring publicly what are their real opinions. There is another document little known and hardly ever published in the English language, to which I call the particular attention of English readers. This is the programme of the "Narodnaia Volia's party," which until now practically represented what may be called "Nihilism." I will only quote some extracts showing the main points of this programme.

"I. By our general convictions," so runs this document, "we are socialists and democrats. We are convinced that only on socialistic grounds humanity can become the embodiment of freedom, equality, fraternity, securing for itself the general prosperity and the full and harmonious development of man and social progress. We are convinced, moreover, that only the *will of the nation* should give sanction to any social institution, and the development of the nation may be called sound only when independent and free, and when every idea which is to receive practical application has previously passed the test of the national understanding and national will.

"II. We think, therefore, that as socialists and democrats we must recognise, as our immediate purpose, the liberation of the nation from the oppression of the present state by making a political revolution with the object of transferring the supreme power into the hands of the nation.

"III. We think that the will of the nation should be sufficiently clearly expressed and applied by a National Assembly, freely elected by the vote of all citizens, and provided with instruction from their electors. This we do not consider to be the ideal form of the manifestation of the will of the nation, but it is the only one practically realisable, and we feel bound, therefore, to accept it.

"IV. Submitting ourselves completely to the will of the nation, we, as a party, feel bound to appear before the country with our own programme, which we shall propagate before the revolution, recommending it to the electors during the electoral periods, and which we shall defend in the National Assembly. This programme consists of the following heads :—

"1. The permanent representative Assembly to have the supreme control and direction in all general State questions.

"2. Large provincial self-government, secured by the election of all public functionaries.

"3. Independence of the village commune ('Mir') as an economical and administrative unit.

"4. Nationalisation of land.

"5. Series of measures tending to transfer the possession of fabrics to workmen.

"6. Complete liberty of conscience, speech, press, meetings, associations, and electoral agitation.

"7. Extension of the right to vote to all citizens having attained full age, without any class or wealth distinctions.

"8. Substitution of a standing army by a territorial militia."

I have faithfully translated the essential parts of the Narodnaia Volia's programme, omitting only some repetitions and the explanatory paragraphs.

II.

The hope or desire to reduce a successful revolution into a vast electoral comity, and nothing more, can hardly be realised in practice, however sincere may be the desire of its initiators. If we want to know what a political revolution will do, we must inquire into the practical aspirations of the elements of the society and of the nation which are likely to take part in it. But this part of the programme is very suggestive and conclusive of the spirit of the party which stood for so many years at the head of the Russian liberation movement.

Since the Nihilists never wanted to force on anybody their private opinions, and proposed to acquire adherents only by means of persuasion, the persecutions to which they are subjected are no longer "the defence of order," but are mere acts of tyranny; just as the religious persecutions were. Every human being has a right to find, according to his taste, the way to social happiness as well as to paradise, and to show it to his fellow-men. No matter whether he is right or wrong, people who hear him will decide for themselves. But the Russian Government will not afford this opportunity, knowing too well that the people's decision will not be in its favour. It tabooed not only socialism, but everything tending to the good of the nation, to progress, and to general liberty. This necessitated a political struggle, and the battle began all along the line. The socialists, recruited from among the well-to-do classes as well as from workmen, were the first to assume the initiative, and remained the most ardent in carrying it through. Was it because they are socialistic? No; socialism in itself has little to do with it. They possessed in the highest degree what urges people to similar struggles: the spirit of self-sacrifice, and the unbounded ardour of serving their country. A pure "liberal," a man believing in political freedom as the ultimate perfection of human society, may unite quite fraternally with their efforts. In one very important instance we may infer that this is no mere abstract possibility. I refer to the numerous adherents the Nihilists have acquired of late in the army. The military officers took hardly any part in the movement when it was in its purely socialistic state. Among the many hundreds of them who fraternised with the revolution since it was directed against autocracy, there must have been of course many officers converted to socialistic ideas, but there is no doubt that the bulk of them sympathised with the revolution out of pure patriotism. And it is to the patriotism of the army that the revolutionists appealed. The fusion of the military patriotic elements and the initiatory socialist is now complete. They make at present one compact body of conspirators, in which the intensity of the pending struggle has put into the background any theoretical divergency. We have full reason to believe that this fusion is extending rapidly to the civilian patriotic elements of our society in general.

Thus we may say that the Nihilist movement, which some fifteen years ago was commenced by a set of young enthusiasts of socialistic creed, now, under the influence of internal causes, and the great spread of disaffection in the country, is tending to transform itself into a vast patriotic revolutionary party, composed of people of various shades of opinions, united in a common effort to destroy a tyranny obnoxious to all. They want to substitute for it a national government, in which all shall possess the possibility of working pacifically for the good of the country. Nothing can be more moderate, more just, nor give them a greater right to say they are working for the common good.

* * * * * *

I will not leave the subject of the general destructive tendencies of the Nihilists without saying some words on one particular point,—the connection of their political creed with religion. Taking advantage of the well-known religiousness of the English, some good friends of the Russian Government are doing their best to spread among them the idea that the Nihilists are striving to destroy all kinds of religion, in order to force on people something like the worship of the Goddess of Reason.

The religious condition of Russia presents some peculiarities which give to the religious policy of the Nihilist a special stamp. That the Nihilists are Atheists is quite true. But to say that they are striving to destroy religion is quite false. First, among the instructed classes of every description, which until now have furnished the largest contingent of revolutionists, there is nothing left to destroy; because among our educated classes Atheism is as general a doctrine as Christianity is in England. It is the national religion of our educated classes, and as such it has already had time to acquire the state of happy indifference, which, according to Thomas Bucle's opinion, is the best guarantee of religious tolerance. In this particular Russia differs greatly from all European countries, Italy and France included. I will not dwell on the causes of this peculiarity, due to the history and present character of our Church. I simply state an undeniable fact.

With the lower classes it is of course different Russian peasants are said to be very religious. That is true in respect to the dissenting sects, but not to official orthodoxy. What really prevails is a mechanical, rather heathenish, Ritualism, under which religious indifference is lurking. A clergy deprived of any independence, controlled at every step, submitted to censorship in every sermon, and drilled to passive submission to the order of the Tzar's officers, could as little answer the religious wants of the peasants as withstand the free-thinking movement of the superior classes. Unable to make any suitable use of mental culture, science, philosophy, and even theology; driven by experience to consider even strong religious zeal as something rather dangerous, as threatening to break the dead somnolence which is the ideal of bureaucratic despotism,— what could such a clergy be but the mere functionaries of religious ceremonies, devoid of any spiritual sense? What moral influence may these mouthpieces of the Government have, speaking at its bidding? Long ago the Russian priests forsook any proud emulation for moral leadership, caring only to extract from the peasants as much money and goods as possible. And the orthodox peasants do not at all respect their voracious exacting priests; and they often despise and ridicule them. But the peasants believe in Jesus Christ, in the Virgin Mary, and in the many saints dividing among themselves the cares of the universe, while the priest is the only possessor of the secrets of propitiating all these heavenly powers by certain ceremonies : St. Vlas, the cattle preserver ; St. Elia, the rain giver ; and St. George, whom the wolves obey. The priest is indispensable for getting good harvests, good flocks, and preserving the fields from drought.* People cannot help recurring to them, however unwilling they may be to pay them the high rate they impose. As to Christian duties, an orthodox peasant thinks himself perfectly acquitted if he baptises his children, weds his daughter in church, and pays the priest for officiating once or twice a year. He goes to church only when it is not too distant and time permits. The best illustration of his religious indifference is the general neglect to communicate, as enjoined by the Church, not less than once a year, although enforced by police regulation. The official reports of country priests show that, in parishes of three or four thousand people, very often no more than two or three hundred take part in this chief manifestation of an orthodox believer's adherence to his Church. And often among the peasants, especially those who are wont to travel, you may meet people, without having a bit of heresy in them, who for ten, fifteen, and twenty years have never been to communion. A religion of this kind is really not worth destroying, if even we had nourished the absurd idea of carrying on a propaganda of Atheism by means of secret societies. All we cared for was to restrain our men from going

* The strong heathenish aspect of Russian orthodoxy is very well noticed and illustrated in Mr. Mackenzie Wallace's " Russia," to which book I refer my readers.

to confession, lest some compromising word should escape them. For, in Russia, a priest hearing in confession anything about political conspiracies, *is bound by law* to break the secret of the confessional; inviolable in case of parricide. This abstinence it was, of course, very easy to obtain on mere practical grounds of expediency. And I may add that the initiative in such a resolution was usually taken by our peasants and workmen converted to the idea of revolution. Into purely theological discussions we never entered with our workmen; it would have diverted their attention from the political and social questions we cared so much about, to others which had for us really no interest at all.

Now some words about the sects. They are extremely numerous. The number of their adherents is not known exactly. Competent specialists reckon at present no less than fifteen millions—about one-fourth of the rural population of Russia proper. But they spread and multiply every day. All the truly religious elements of Russia are comprised in them. If an orthodox peasant awakes from his religious indifference, he unites with some existing sect suiting best his taste, or creates a new one. In those sects religion is no longer a shallow ritualistic observance. It is a living power, inspiring and informing all political and social conceptions of the sectarian; the greatest moral force moving our peasantry. But all these sectarian religions, being inspired by the complex influence of religious discontent, and political and social oppression, have more or less strongly marked oppositionist and anti-governmental tendencies. Some of them strive after the social equality of the primitive Christian; others go so far as to proclaim the emperor to be an anti-Christ, and refuse to recognise any official of his, or to obey any order issued by the Government; flying into the wilderness to avoid taking passports.

Such religions we, of course, had no interest at all in destroying. I will also add, among Russian Nihilists there were many, and the writer of these pages among them, who hoped that those discontented masses might be induced by our propaganda to some active protest. Such attempts, and they were many, extended our sphere of propaganda, but had no serious result. It would lead us too far away to speak fully on this subject. The Russian sects possess in them a great creative power, which undoubtedly will be turned to account when the country shall be free to assert its independence. But their *destructive* power is, I daresay, *nil*. They have displayed an enormous power of passive resistance and self-sacrifice, but there is no way to influence them to an active revolutionary protest against their oppressor.

CHAPTER II.

WHAT ARE THE FORCES THE RUSSIAN REVOLUTION COMMANDS?

I.

"IF a tithe of what is told in this (my last) book be true, the social and political condition of Russia is frightful beyond conception. The autocracy is desperate; the revolution, when it comes, will be terrible," says the *Scotsman*. I abstain from answering this, one of the many uncertain "ifs," because without my stepping into the lists, there appears day by day confirmation of all my statements. The little indecision, very natural before the enormity of the horrors going on in Russia, gives way to the conviction that I have not given to my possible opponents the satisfaction of exaggerating any of my statements. "A careful examination of our author's statements leads us to believe that they possess the characteristic of 'moderation and sobriety' which he claims for them," says the *Westminster Review* for July, after discussing the many documents on Russia English literature possesses. Time will induce, I hope, all my readers to come to an identical conclusion. What I propose here to do is to say something concerning the *Scotsman's* conjectures about the coming revolution, as being very common, and likely to spread with the diffusion of knowledge about the real condition of Russia.

Is the coming Russian revolution likely to be as dreadful as the horrors of the Russian *régime* induce us to expect?

Surely a revolution in St. Petersburg, when it happens, cannot help being very energetic. But it is not this which people generally mean. The common idea of the probable Russian revolution is that of a universal cataclysm, in which the long-repressed hatred and revenge of the masses will find at last free play. It is, in a word, a popular or peasants' revolution. No categorical answer is possible, of course, on the question of its probability. I will only point out that the peasants' revolution, in various times, was the object of many misconceptions. Judging by the general devotion of Russian peasants to the Tzar, many observers, especially of foreign origin, have sincerely expressed their conviction that as long as this sentiment maintains its vigour, the existing order of things is exposed to no danger, and all exertions of the Nihilists will be set at nought. On the other hand, among the Nihilists of the first period, there were many who pointed out the unmistakable hatred of Russian peasants to all institutions which practically embody what is called "the State," and "the social order," concluding that the peasants were capable of rising in arms against their oppressors at the first opportunity, as their forefathers did under the leadership of Pugatcheff, and Stenko Rasin.

Both opinions are, I think, quite erroneous. The

traditional monarchism of Russian peasants, though greatly diminished during the last twenty years, is nevertheless a notorious element in our peasants' ethics. But it would be quite wrong to consider it as a general preservative against disturbances, rebellions, or even revolution. People are prone to picture things of other countries after their own pattern. If the English know, for example, that their countrymen are full of reverence and confidence in the Prime Minister who is governing the country, they can surely consider it as a perfect guarantee for the maintenance of order. But it is wholly different with Russia and its Tzar, or, I daresay, with any autocrat and his faithful peasants. For the agricultural classes of all despotisms, scarcely differing in ignorance, are everywhere too short-sighted to pierce, by their intellectual eyes, through the thick hierarchy of officers, and see what their sovereign really is. Nonsense about the fatherly disposition of the king was most common among the French peasants in the epoch of the Great Revolution. The German peasants of the sixteenth century, followers of Münster, whilst burning castles and putting to torture and death hundreds of nobles, professed allegiance to the emperor, and in their well-known manifestoes desired the emperor alone to rule them. And the Ruthenian peasants, who perpetrated the Galician massacres in 1846, proclaimed themselves, and really were, most devoted partisans of His Austrian Majesty.

If the Russian peasants, whose feelings toward the officers of the State and the representatives of privileged classes are hardly more friendly, begin one fine morning to burn the noblemen's houses, and destroy landlords, policemen, administrators, the thing will be no worse and no better whether they shout all the while "Long live the Tzar!" or not. A peasant revolution can very easily burst out in the present mental condition of the Russian peasants. There is no need to wait until they lose their monarchism, nor is this monarchism a security against the possibility of insurrection. If order is preserved, it means that they have not yet lost patience; that is all. But nobody can guarantee that they will not lose it to-morrow. Ideas find their way into the minds of illiterate masses very slowly. But feelings and passions spread like wildfire. A general famine, which in the present state of misery would be something awful, a disastrous war, obliging the State to augment the taxes or to overstrain the conscriptions, might cause disturbances to arise spontaneously in many places, and there is no saying what might happen.

But leaving the future to the future, and judging with cool heads about the present, we say that there is no visible sign of the imminence of such a catastrophe. True, agrarian crimes grow rather frequent. Serious agrarian disturbances, assuming sometimes the character of organised armed rebellions, and lasting many months, occur in a number of places. The wild outbursts against the Jews, embracing one-half of Russia, could not happen in a well-balanced State. All these are serious signs; but when the time is ripe, something far more serious will be seen. The peasants' revolution—the sweeping, all-destructive, barbarous revolution—is in the background. The revolution of to-day is a town revolution, which is quickly approaching. For the great intellectual evolutions of our time, being very slow to work in the villages, acquire a wonderful energy and thoroughness in our towns, where they pervade not only the upper, but also the lower classes.

II.

In every country considerable difference is observable between town and village life—the people of the town being always much quicker to accept innovations both in their customs and in the domain of intellect. In Russia, however, this difference is greater than elsewhere, owing to the social condition and the family life of our peasants. The type of the peasant families is strictly patriarchal. Only the independent Ruthenians are accustomed when married to establish separate households. The Russian peasant generally does not separate from his paternal home, all the members living together in very large families, composed of two or three successive generations, under the despotic rule of the head of the household, numbering sometimes ten to fifteen or more male and female workpeople. Such families are very advantageous from an economical point of view, being a kind of productive and consuming associations. But family despotism, the complete dependence of the women and younger members upon the stubborn will of the elderly " head-man," is one of the greatest evils of our country life. Besides, as only the independent householders have the right to assist in the village assembly, it follows as a result that a considerable part of the full-grown population is practically excluded from having any voice in the management of local affairs. Then village self-government in a country ruled by ruthless bureaucratic despotism, where nothing is known about individual dignity and independence, has naturally outstepped its limit, and become in many cases a sort of patriarchal tutorship. The Russian "Mir" interferes with the private life of its members in a manner that would never be suffered by a man of Saxon origin, while the Russian peasants bear this dependency with the utmost submission, accustomed as they are to consider the "Mir" as their only refuge and protector. In such a condition it would be surprising if the Russian peasantry were less conservative, less patriarchal than they are. And the part of the community which always is the most liable to be influenced by progressive ideas—the young generation—in our villages is precisely that which lacks any independence of spirit; nay, any interest in questions of general character. If you are a propagandist going "among the peasants," do not follow the traditional precept of addressing new ideas to the new generations. You will be entirely disappointed and dispirited by their utter frivolity. You must win the ear of their elders, who in the villages seem to have engrossed the intellectual activity and the social instincts of the whole community.

But go among the workmen of the towns, and you will be struck by a perfect contrast. Our towns possessed until lately comparatively few professional workmen. The majority of hands in our manufactories consist of peasants whose families live in some far distant village. If the workman cannot afford to go home even for a holiday, or the summer season, he brings his wife in town, but continues to hold a share in the land of the family. In nine cases out of ten peasants going into the town are people occupying subordinate positions in the household. The "head man" never abandons the land unless he is totally ruined. Usually he sends a younger member of the family, his son or younger brother, to town to make up the money required for taxes. The young people are, most of them, very anxious to go to the towns. It is a sort of emancipation from their dependent position at home. There is no "elder" to command him, no "old people" whose will is a law and guidance for him. He is a full-grown, independent man, responsible for his conduct, and bound to think for himself and those whom he has left at home. He has new cares, new interests; his mental activity is at once awakened. The stream of new impressions, conceptions, observations, rushing on him from every part, do not slide any more from his intellect without touching it. He is in the fittest disposition to accept everything new that strikes him, and the memory of his past dependence makes him only the more inclined to do so. As to the old ideas carried from home, they have no strong hold on him, being associated with a standard of life and culture he cannot help now thinking are backward, and sometimes ridiculous. An intelligent young peasant coming for the first time into a town is really in a position somewhat similar to that of a young man or girl of the well-to-do classes fresh in the capital from some remote little town or country house. The workman's mental field of activity is certainly limited, for he is generally illiterate, as the majority of Russian peasants are, but he is the more easily impressed by the less comprehensive but more subtle vehicle of speech.

The seed of revolution thrown by zealous hands on such a ground must have produced a very good harvest. We may add that the sowing itself was much easier in the towns than in the villages. An intelligent man, a new-comer, settled in a village, whether he be a schoolmaster, or communal clerk, or an artisan, becomes at once the object of general curiosity. All eyes are strictly kept on him. No step, no word of his passes unnoticed in the patriarchal drowsiness of village life, and the police have, of course, full knowledge of it. But in the busy swarming of great towns no police superintendence can impede frequent intercourse among people, provided they do not neglect to take some precautions. And a good deal of time will elapse before the spies catch any hints of the suspicious visits of a poorly dressed student to the house of some workman. Finally, there is not so great an abyss between workmen and the representatives of the well-to-do classes as between the latter and the peasants. They are both towns-people; they are in immediate contact with the representatives of the authorities; they feel the vexations and wrongs inflicted by the despotism of the police. And to facilitate mutual understanding there is an infinite variety of gradation between the workpeople of the towns, the skilled labourers living continually in the towns, presenting by their intellectual development little, if any, difference with the workmen of any great capital.

To show what the revolutionary propaganda accomplished among workmen, let us stop a moment in St. Petersburg. The revolutionists of 1860 and 1866 had some adherents among the working people of St. Petersburg and Moscow, but with the destruction of organisations all connection between revolutionists and workpeople was broken, and the present generation had to begin anew. The first attempts to do something among working men were made at St. Petersburg about 1871, and it happened that the propaganda was chiefly addressed to the unskilled labourers, forming the bulk of the working class of the capital. To give an idea of the primitive state of their political conceptions, suffice it to relate the curious difficulty we propagandists encountered in our first steps, when, after some chatting in plebeian tea-rooms, we succeeded sufficiently in becoming acquainted with a number of intelligent workmen to invite them to our lodging to talk more freely about politics. Some called on us, but many who promised did not come. We suspected it was out of fear of the police, but it was not so. The fact was, that some of the propagandists were medical students, and the workmen having vaguely heard, not without superstitious dread, of the dissection of corpses made in the Anatomical Hall, the rumour spread among them that the "students" inviting the workmen for a mysterious interview planned for nothing less than to murder them and to carry their bodies secretly to the dissecting-room. The more timid were afraid, and abstained from coming. When, however, they saw that nothing of the kind happened, and their companions returned from the dangerous visits safe and sound, they grew emboldened, and came more freely. But for a long time they were unable to understand what on earth those visits meant. They were so ignorant of politics that they could not conceive how the simple talking about the poverty of the peasants, the unjust distribution of taxes, and so forth, might be an object of importance in itself. The propagandists, in order to facilitate the acquirement of social knowledge for their disciples, taught them to read. The workmen thought that we were simply good-hearted schoolmasters out of employment. Many of them went so far as to offer us money spontaneously, as some remuneration for our trouble. And when we categorically declined, the workmen were quite puzzled, and decided among themselves that it was the Tzar who ordered these good men and women to give instruction to workmen, and to tell them the truth about everything, and that he would recompense the propagandists by giving them medals for doing this act of kindness. All this we learned later from the mouths of our friends the workmen of the Vyborg and Petersburg side district, in which the propaganda was initiated, when they became really converted to our ideas, and understood the meaning of what we taught them. Of course not all the St. Petersburg workmen were so ingenuous, but the great majority was undoubtedly not so much in advance of such antediluvian ideas.

Ten years passed, and the political physiognomy of the St. Petersburg workmen changed completely. Save some stripling quite new from his village, it became difficult to meet with an average workman who did not know what revolution meant. And among those who knew there were few who did not sympathise with it. Many read the revolutionary periodical, or kept in their small chests revolutionary pamphlets. On the whole, we may affirm, without exaggeration, that the workmen of St. Petersburg at present are no less imbued with revolutionary ideas than the youth of the educated classes, and in all the trials of the last period (save the military ones), among the accused there was always a very large percentage of workmen. This striking change was wrought not by the propaganda only. With the best zeal and greatest ability of the propagandists it would be impossible to work such a miracle. We must remember that in Russia there is no opportunity for influencing the masses. We cannot convene large meetings, nor throw our pamphlets and papers to the four winds of heaven. To shake the secular torpor of the Russian masses we had nothing but the whisper, the secret propaganda addressed with circumspection to private men. Such a propaganda is too inadequate for its task. To rouse the spirit of our masses deeds were required; words served only to explain and bring home to people's understanding that which had struck their mind and excited their spirit. The great change in the political atmosphere of St. Petersburg is chiefly due to the mighty struggle with the Autocracy, carried on for so many years by the Nihilists, naturally impressing most strongly the population of the town which was the chief scene of their activity. The feeling of amazement passed over, curiosity succeeded, and in the capital the means of satisfying it being always at hand, the vague sympathy which working people always feel for courage and pluck turned quickly into conscious partisanship. The longer the struggle lasted the greater was the wonder and admiration for the strugglers, and the stronger the sympathy with the cause they championed. And the secret adherents of the revolutionary organisation were always there ready to add fuel to this common sentiment, to remove objections, and to enlist in their ranks the most prominent and zealous among their sympathisers. Revolutionary organisations, composed of workmen, quite conscious of their revolutionary ends and means, had taken the place of the clumsy gatherings, half school, half club, of the period of 1871-74. Police persecutions began; hundreds of workmen were arrested, imprisoned, exiled. But the movement grew in extent and intensity, embracing new districts, spreading to other towns. As an example, I will mention that in the time of Kalturins' leadership (1879-80), for which I have positive data, the St. Petersburg workmen's organisation, known under the name of the Northern Workmen's League, was composed of about 200 to 300 members, divided into about fifteen to twenty groups, working in various quarters of the capital, having their regular secret meetings, their own finances, and their central governing committee to dispose of the material means and the *personnel* of the organisation. Such a force will seem very small to a member of an English trade union numbering many thousands. But it must be remembered that with secret revolutionary organisations it is quite different than with public and pacific ones. There are thousands of considerations unknown to the latter, which a revolutionary organisation must take into account before admitting a man into its ranks. One imprudent member may ruin in no time all which has been done during years of incessant and perilous toil. A secret society can only accept a small part of those who would be willing to enter it. It is not the body of the party, as it is with a public association, but only its nerves and sinews which, ramified among the large body of sympathisers, can in the decisive moment give it the required impulse.

In November 1879, when the violent death of seven workmen at the explosion of the cartridge manufactory of Vasiliostrov gave occasion for a revolutionary manifestation, the Northern League, though then in infancy, could lead into the street no less than ten to twelve thousand workmen. In the case of a barricade struggle, a well-selected organisation of 200 to 300 conspirators, having its ramifications in all the principal manufactories, can lead into the streets the bulk of the working population of an enormous town, provided the revolutionary feeling has a strong hold over the masses.

The St. Petersburg workmen are much in advance compared with those of the other towns; just as in France, in Germany, and other countries where the centralisation of the strength of the Government calls out naturally a similar concentration of revolutionary forces and exertions. But in all the principal towns the seed of disaffection is sufficiently spread to render them very " unsafe " for the Government, especially in the large towns of South and Western Russia.* In 1879 Prince Dmitry Kropotkin (cousin of Peter Kropotkin), then Governor-General of the province of Kharkoff, in his secret annual report to the Emperor, which the Nihilists succeeded in obtaining and publishing, says plainly, that though in the country the efforts of the propagandists have not produced serious damage, in the towns it was quite the reverse, and he can no more answer for the faithfulness of the working population of Kharkoff. So it is in many other principal Russian towns. The conversion of so many workmen to revolutionary ideas is undoubtedly one of the most important and most useful services performed by the revolutionist of the present generation. The idea of liberty, the hatred to autocracy, is no more the exclusive patrimony of the superior classes, as it was formerly. These ideas are brought now to the heart of the masses, and nothing can prevent them continually oozing out from the towns' workpeople to the agricultural classes. Often wanting system, and leaving little deposit in the form of permanent

* A revolutionary organisation quite similar in its tendencies to the Northern League was created in 1879-80 in South Russia (Kieff, Odessa, Kharkoff), under the name of the Southern Workmen's League. It possessed a printing office, and issued at various times many revolutionary proclamations. But I have no particular information as to its numerical strength and organisation.

organisation, the propaganda among the town labourers was carried on uninterruptedly all the time by a considerable number of people. The amount of intellectual change wrought by it is very great. And I am glad to state that lately a noticeable revival of this activity manifested itself in the ranks of the Russian Nihilists, and a numerous and growing body of people have accepted the propaganda among workmen as their chief aim.

Taking all this into account,—the general disaffection of the town population, and the facility afforded to the creation of revolutionary organisations among them,—we are fully entitled to conclude that if Russian towns were as large as those of Western Europe, and had formed so considerable a quota of the population as in France, England, or Germany, we could fairly have hope in town revolutions like those of Paris, Vienna, and Milan. But, unhappily, it is not so. Russian industrial development is very rapid, it is true, but it is due chiefly to the improvement in the mode of production. The number of hands employed by our manufacturers grows very slowly. The capital which bears so strongly on the destinies of a centralised state in Russia forms less than $\frac{1}{100}$th, whilst Paris forms about $\frac{1}{7}$th of the whole population of the country. In the insurrection of 1878 in Milan, a town of 200,000 inhabitants, it had to struggle against 40,000 of Radezki's battalions, and Milan won the battle. Paris, with its two and a half millions, was under still more favourable conditions. And that great town has won many times, having been able to struggle with forces more or less equalised with those opposing them. Whilst in

St. Petersburg there are two soldiers for every workman, and in the case of the prolongation of street fighting for a few days there would be twice as many : in such conditions a purely civil insurrection is hopeless. The only insurrection having a chance of success in Russia is that which combines the advantages of surprise with energy ; an insurrection which paralyses the whole governmental machine by striking from within, while, in the meantime, other forces are attacking it from without. The Revolution, in a word, must have adherents among those who stand near the very centre of the Government ; those who are the nominal supporters of the Autocracy—the army.

How far is this prospect likely to be realised ?

III.

Russians, waking up to political life, began by the insurrection of the Decembrist, in which the flower of the army took part. The military could not surely have a nobler tradition to inspire them, nor better examples to follow. In the epoch of the revival of intellectual and Liberal movement which followed the Crimean war, we see the military taking no less a part in it than the professors, students, *littérateurs*, etc. There were Liberal clubs composed of officers of all arms, and it is a well-known fact that the chief office for the reprint and distribution of *Kolokol* (Herzen's clandestine paper) was organised by the Military Academy of the general staff. The names of generals and colonels are connected with secret societies, and dozens of officers of every grade are condemned to Siberia to imprisonment for life, and to death for their revolutionary sympathies.

When, in 1870, ten years later, the socialistic rush of the young people "among the peasants" began, the officers, as such, could not take part in it. But even this movement had an echo with the officers of the army. About a score of them, chiefly of younger grade, but also some of a higher rank, abandoned the service, and united with the propagandists. The military, in a word, was always susceptible to the influence coming from the exterior world. And there is nothing surprising in this. The staff of Russian officers differs greatly from what people are wont to associate with the idea of a military caste. They are the direct contrast to the stiff-necked Prussian younker, the ideal of a modern soldier, who is proud of his noble origin, proud of his uniform and traditional devotion to the king; who is enacting his drilling manœuvre with the earnestness of an officiating clergyman; who despises most sincerely all which is not rendered sacred by a brazen casque or a bottle-green overcoat. The Russian military officers are plain and unassuming men, with no sentiment of inborn superiority of origin, as such feeling is little known among the Russian nobility to which they belong. They possess neither particular devotion nor hostility to the existing *régime*. Russians, unless they begin to conspire, have little opportunity of thinking seriously about politics, and the general colour of political opinions of all official classes is that of indifference. Neither have they any special attachment to the profession they have adopted. They become military officers as they might become magistrates, surgeons, or agriculturists, because when still of tender age their parents send them to military instead of civilian schools. And they remain in the profession imposed on them, since a man must serve somewhere to get his living, and the military career, after all, is neither worse nor better than any other. Besides, they are doing their best to smooth that life, devoting to military duties as little time and trouble as possible. They are, of course, eager for promotion, but prefer to get their advancement remaining in their slippers and dressing-gown. They do not read professional books, and if they are subscribers *ex officio* to a military magazine, you will see it uncut often for years. If reading anything at all, it is the current literature, especially our great popular monthly magazine, supplying with intellectual food our young generation. And among the young officers of distant regiments or batteries there are partisans of some popular author or the other, and discussions on political and social questions are held as warm as those among the undergraduates of a university. Military "jingoism" is quite unknown among our officers. If you hear of an officer who is raving about his bloody profession, or who has a passion for drilling exercises, you may bet twenty to one that he is a blockhead.

With such a staff of officers an army is not destined perhaps to develop to the utmost its aggressive qualities, but it leaves it open to all humanitarian and really patriotic influences; it makes an irremovable obstacle to its turning to a lasting instrument of oppression of the country. Every Liberal movement will find supporters and adherents in its ranks. And to return to our subject, so it was with the present phase of the Russian Revolution. From the epoch when the Nihilists entered resolutely into the fierce battle of Autocracy, their adherents among the officers grew very rapidly, extending from the capital over all Russia. In 1881-2, when the first conspiracy was discovered by treason, the police made about two hundred arrests among military officers of all grades and all arms. The traces of conspiracy were discovered in fourteen among the greatest military centres of Russia, such as St. Petersburg, Cronstradt, Odessa, Nikolaieff. The judicial inquiry has brought out the fact that the military were united in a conspiracy, with the determined purpose of helping the open insurrection intended to overthrow the Autocracy. They had a central directing committee, having its seat at St. Petersburg, and composed of few members, officers of the garrison of the capital and of the navy of Cronstradt. By the care of their emissaries they founded conspiracy groups among the officers of other towns. The trial of October 1884, the only one which the Government had the courage to hold (all the rest of the military being sentenced to various penalties without judgment), has shown that really the best and noblest of Russia's sons are uniting in the name of its freedom. And they are no longer young people; for among the first stand the names of such men as Lieutenant-Colonel Ashenbrenner, a warrior of forty years of age, and with twenty years' military service, the hero of the Central Asian War, who won a dozen military distinctions—crosses, medals, swords of honour, promotions, and honourable mention—by his splendid courage in many battles, in storming fortresses and towns. In his mature age he became one of the most resolute champions of the Revolution, converting to it half a score of the officers of his regiment, founding military groups in other regiments, sending emissaries to far distant towns, and himself making propagandist journeys through Russia. There is also the brilliant artillery officer, Captain Pochitonov, hero of the Turkish War, who distinguished himself in many battles and difficult passages, sieges, and stormings, who returned home laden with honours and distinctions, finishing his career with distinguished success at the Artillery Academy, and entered the ranks of the conspirators, becoming most active in propagating the Revolution among them. There are Captain Rogachief, Baron Stromberg, the naval officer, commander of the Pacific Squadron—all people to whom their very enemies were obliged to give credit for their merit. When such as these declare unanimously before the tribunal that the best service they felt bound in honour to render to their country was to unite with the enemy of the Government to which they had sworn fidelity, this is an emphatical proof that such a Government has become the worst enemy of the country.

It is quite evident that the adherents of the Revolution among the army in the epoch we are speaking of are not to be trifled with. Numerically, as well as morally, they represented a force which really promised to occasion serious trouble to the Russian Tzars. In a strongly constituted healthy state the material forces represented by the conspiracies of 1881-2 would be ridiculously insufficient. But it is quite different in Russia. Despotic states in general have little power of resistance against internal enemies. The concentration of all governmental functions to one centre leaves the whole body politic helpless, if the blow is adroitly struck at the head. This explains the notorious fact of the facility with which success was obtained by the Palace revolutions in many despotisms, including Russia of the eighteenth century, when a handful of body guards exalted and dethroned Tzars and Tzarinas. *That* is no longer likely to happen. If the Autocracy arrive at such a condition of decomposition that ambitious generals should aspire to Prætorian revolution, they will undoubtedly hoist some political banner to get support and conceal their private aims. But against liberatory insurrection the Russian Autocracy is no better guaranteed than against the Palace revolution in the past century. We must remember that the great Decembrist insurrection had few battalions under its command, and it imperilled most seriously the throne of Nicholas I., and might indeed have overthrown it, were it not for the want of resolution in the leaders. From early morning until 4 P.M. the soldiers stood on the Winter Palace Square before the quasi-defenceless palace, waiting vainly for the Dictator, who had disappeared, to lead them to the assault. Nobody took his place, and Nicholas I. consequently had full time to assemble his troops and demolish his enemy with grape-shot.

True, the military conspiracy of which we are speaking now was much inferior to that of the Decembrists. Though having the best reason to count upon the immediate support of workmen and the bulk of the educated classes, it was not sufficient to raise the banner of insurrection. But it had collected such considerable forces in so short a time, and was spreading so quickly, that the best hopes were entertained for the next few years.

But the bright prospects of the conspiracy were blighted. Owing to the vilest of treason the military organisation was discovered. Hundreds of officers were arrested, to be either imprisoned, shot, hanged, or exiled, together with many hundreds of civilians and workmen.

We may admit, as a rule, if the conspiracy had once obtained a given result, this example would have been an additional chance for obtaining the same next time, provided the general conditions remained unchanged. I hardly need to add that not all the military conspirators were arrested. There still are plenty to continue the work. And one of those conspirators, speaking for all his companions, has recently published in *Narodnaia Volia Messenger* a long letter, intended to answer the numerous accusations made against the military conspirators by their adversaries. Alarmed by the great spread of revolution among the officers, the Government nominated a Commission of Inquiry, composed of generals, ministers, and grand dukes. But those personages, in their high wisdom, concluded that the cause which induced the officers to unite with the Revolution was their bad pay and slow promotion! In high society and the military circles of St. Petersburg people said that all the evil proceeded from the devilish cunning of the revolutionist, who ensared hundreds of officers, employing for this purpose female propagandists. No! answered the author of this interesting letter, there is no need of ensnaring nor of meeting with a revolutionary emissary for converting an officer to an adherent of revolution at present. The chief agent of conversion is the part which the Government forces the officer to play; the principal cause of discontent is the degradation of the functions laid on the modern military officer. "Imagine," he says, "a model officer, who has never troubled himself about politics, or read political books, but who is endowed with natural good sense, and think to what conclusions he must come in the execution of such duties as this. Strikes have lately grown common; and if they become serious the troops are always called out to 'restore order'—in other words, to force workmen to abandon their demands, however moderate, and to submit to all which the masters wish to inflict on them. If the men call a meeting to discuss their grievances, the troops disperse them, sometimes by force of arms, but no objection is raised to the meetings and discussions of the masters and their friends. The peasants, to take another instance, refuse to pay taxes—an event common enough of late. The 'stanovi' (chief of the district police) comes in order to realise the amount due by selling their effects. The peasants will not suffer the auction to proceed.

It is a 'rebellion;' the troops are called in and set to work. They shoot down, slay, and make prisoners. The enemy is vanquished and surrenders. The leaders are bound and sent to prison for more severe punishment. The rest receive patriarchal correction; they are knouted in a body, from the beardless boy to the white-haired grandfather. After the general flagellation the stock and chattels of the conquered are sold up, and the victors are quartered for some weeks in the houses of the vanquished, to consume, in the way of punishment, the last crust left them after the auction. In the excitement of the struggle our officer has no time to think. But now the struggle is over, and he looks round him with surprise. He knows military history, and has read of wars with savage tribes, but he has never heard that it is a conqueror's business to flog and starve his defeated foes. The officer is curious to know something more of this same enemy—the very peasant so beloved of the Tzar and the *Tchinovniks*. He has time and opportunity for his studies now that he is billeted in the peasants' houses. He finds that the so-called rebellion was an act of sheer despair. The peasants had not a farthing to pay the taxes, which exceeded their whole income. They resisted the sale of their cattle, because they cannot till the land without them, and famine must follow their loss. The officer is forced to own with shame he has played the part, not of a soldier, but of a gendarme and executioner. Take another case. The Dissenters have built a chapel of their own, and will not permit the police to close it. The *Uniats*, converted to orthodoxy in the bishop's reports, and in them alone, continue to go to the Roman Catholic Church. In both instances the troops are called out with unavoidable results—a struggle, followed by general knouting, and the billeting of troops on the offenders.

" And the escort duties to Siberia, and the prison guard ? What subjects for reflection these must give ! What victims of political and religious persecution he may find in his keeping ! And the orders of the Government when revolution was expected, and the guards were put under the command of the police ? No, gentlemen," continues the writer, " it is not the cunning of revolutionary propagandists that urges us to side with the Revolution ; it is the Government itself—the Government which every hour makes its officers, gaolers, executioners, gendarmes, the servants of every swindler.

" Every officer entering the service takes an oath of fidelity to the Tzar and the country. But is he pledged to serve the Tzar as representing the country, or to serve the country because it is the property of the Tzar ? When the Tzar and the country are at open war, which side should an officer take ? 'If you want to side with the country,' answer the partisans of the inviolability of military discipline, ' if you want to conspire, quit the service. You are not forced to wear the uniform. You serve by your own wish. Unless you resign your commission you must do what you are paid for.' Yes, and such a step would be quite reasonable did the army consist of officers alone. The malcontents would throw up their commissions, and organise themselves as a revolutionary force. They would give battle to their comrades who remained true to the Government, and the issue would be settled once for all. But the difficulty is that the officers who remain true to the Government will have over a million of soldiers under their orders—over a million of soldiers who are forced to serve, and cannot resign; while the officers who side with the nation will not be allowed to engage soldiers or recruits."

I have transcribed these paragraphs because they are an authentic expression of the feelings and ideas of those military conspirators. Nothing could be more suited to give us a better assurance for the future. We may fairly hope that the Russian Revolution, once having begun this way, will proceed in the direction of open insurrection. It is the promptest, the surest,—and however energetic it be,—the most human means to get rid of the present abhorrent system. And I know that among Englishmen this new phase of our revolutionary movement will meet with much greater sympathy than the former one. But I prefer to be quite frank. The difficulties Russian revolutionists have to cope with are enormous. With a much stronger tyranny against us than the Italian, whose struggle for liberty was the direst, we have to organise, on the soil of the enemy in a country swarming with spies, what the Italian patriots could prepare on friendly ground. Such work presents incalculable perils and difficulties, and the further the conspiracy extends the greater is the danger of its discovery. The revolutionary organisation may incorporate once more hundreds of the military and thousands of civilians, and this only to be ruthlessly destroyed in its bloom, to rise anew and once more be destroyed; the dreadful test being repeated again and again before arriving at the glorious and longed-for day of open battle.

Now, will the Russian revolutionists persevere in the purely insurrectional way, without wincing or chafing, readjusting again and again the broken thread, unmoved by the enormity of their losses, or by the absence of palpable results? It may be so, but nobody can wager that so it will be. Russian people, though born in an icy country, are very nervous and excitable. The word of "terrorism" was already uttered by the most popular of our clandestine periodicals, and it will be not at all surprising if we hear now and then of violent attempts against the persons of various representatives of the Government. It is a dreadful thing to take in one's own hands to decide the life or death of men whose guilt would be better judged by the country. But it is the greatest injustice to set against Russian patriots as an accusation what is their dire necessity. No man or woman living in political conditions so entirely different from the Russian has a right to condemn them before knowing what these conditions are. And no Russian, however moderate he be, who knows and feels for the wrongs of his country, *has* condemned them in the past, nor will ever condemn them in the future.

Here is a sample of Russian judgment and a poetical epitome of the deeply tragical position of Russians devoted to their country, expressed by the pen of our great novelist, Ivan Turgueneff, in his " verses in prose," under the title,

"THE THRESHOLD.

" I see a huge building, in the front wall a narrow door, which is wide open ; beyond it stretches a dismal darkness. Before the high threshold stands a girl—a Russian girl.

" The impenetrable darkness is breathing frost, and with the icy breeze from the depth of the building a slow, hollow voice is coming.

" ' O you! wanting to cross this threshold, do you know what awaits you ? '

" ' I know it,' answers the girl.

" ' Cold, hunger, hatred, derision, contempt, insults, prison, suffering, even death ? '

" ' I know it.'

" ' Complete isolation, alienation from all ? '

" ' I know it. I am ready. I will bear all sorrow and miseries.'

" ' Not only if inflicted by enemies, but by kindred and friends ? '

" ' Yes, even by them.'

" ' Well, are you ready for self-sacrifice ? '

" ' Yes.'

" ' For an anonymous self-sacrifice ? You shall die, and nobody, nobody shall know even whose memory is to be honoured.'

" ' I want neither gratitude nor pity. I want no name.'

" ' Are you ready—for a crime ? '

" The girl bent her head.

" ' I am ready even for a crime.'

" The voice paused awhile before renewing its questioning

"'Do you know,' it said at last, 'that you may lose your faith in what you believe now; that you might come to feel that you were mistaken, and have lost in vain your young life?'

"'I know that also. And, nevertheless, I will enter.'

"'Enter then!'

"The girl crossed the threshold, and a heavy curtain fell behind her.

"'A fool!' gnashed some one outside.

"'A saint!' answered a voice from somewhere."

This vision is not to be found of course in the censured edition of Ivan Turgueneff's work. It appeared in the clandestine press, and Mr. P. Lavroff, to whom "The Threshold" was read by the author in the summer of 1882, at Baujival, bears testimony to its fidelity to the original.

CHAPTER III.

WHY RUSSIA IS A CONQUERING COUNTRY.

I.

FOR good or for evil Russia must be a powerful State in Europe and in Asia. A country with one hundred millions of inhabitants, increasing, moreover, with extreme rapidity, cannot be a second-rate power, however badly it be administered. And the seemingly insatiable greed of the Russian empire for territorial extension is not calculated to allay the natural apprehension of its neighbours— of the English more especially, on account of their vast Asiatic dominion. Quite recently this gave rise to the Afghan difficulty, which came within appreciable distance of a *casus belli*, and though the dispute is settled for the present, the political sky is far from being clear. The storm-cloud, laden with war and bloodshed, is hanging over the horizon, arousing much more anxiety than the storm-cloud of possible Russian revolution. Having already investigated the component elements of the latter, let us endeavour to do the same with the former.

Why is Russia a conquering country? What causes this unhappy nation to play the ignoble part of a continual disturber of the tranquillity and peaceful development of countries to which it owes nothing but gratitude for such glimpses of culture and intellectual development as it possesses? The fundamental cause of this is perfectly understood in Europe: it is the existence of Autocracy in Russia. A free government does not exclude the possibility of wars, as the example of Europe has unfortunately shown too well. But in the autocratic States the ambition and cupidity of the masters is a weighty and an additional cause of strife. And the overpowering strength of Russia, together with its geographical position, is particularly adapted to give full play to such propensities of its rulers. Russia alone among European countries is a conquering State in these days. Of late the total ruin of the moral prestige of the Government, and the growing disaffection among all classes of society, has converted into a sort of moral necessity what formerly was a mere luxury. The Tzar must look on external wars as an oft-tried expedient to divert the storm of public discontent from internal questions. The European writers who admit it, ascribe, however, too exclusive an influence in this matter to purely Nihilistic disturbances. This is not quite correct. The Nihilist plots play a comparatively modest part in inducing the Government to look for such expedients, simply because the Nihilists are not so easily diverted from their work. Much more important is the hopeless discontent of the main mass of society, of all who have no share in the plunder and revelry of the dominant clique. The Government must give some occupation to the public mind, lest this dismal uneasiness turn into keen disaffection. And what is very remarkable and characteristic of the present intellectual condition of the Russian people, is the fact that the public opinion of this most pacific of all countries seems at first sight to possess an easily excitable jingoism, making such criminal expedients particularly easy. Whenever there is some diplomatic complication, and some smell of powder in the air, the Russian press seems as if intoxicated all at once with a warlike spirit, and provided the trouble lasts for some time, society seems to be ablaze. Much is to be attributed, of course, to the servile position of the press and the exclusive monopoly of public platforms for the expression of official views. When the Government gives a signal, there are dozens of papers ready to take the hint, and cheer for war as they would have cheered for peace, at the bidding of the authorities. But all is not due to the influence of the police. There are many people who unite in the general chorus spontaneously, and often brawl the loudest, without being in the least "jingoes" at heart. It seems strange, but it is true. I have known such cases myself, and all Russians have witnessed many unexpected transformations into fiery jingoes of very mild and reasonable people. They are simply moved by the unbearable wretchedness of their daily existence ; by the desperate feeling, sometimes unconscious, sometimes quite conscious, that as things cannot be made *worse*, every change is likely to be for the better They welcome with reckless indifference every event even seeming calamity; everything, in a word, provided it promises a violent shock to the unendurable system, no matter how disastrous be the crash. To arrive at such sentiments, men must be driven to madness by continued depression of spirit. And so they really are in Russia. The fact I am alluding to is undeniable, and recurs at every threatened war. It was so in 1883, when a war with Germany was in the air, and also during the last Afghan dispute. And half, if not more, of the so-called "national" excitement which preceded the Bulgarian War, had precisely the same source. This patriotic uproar has, of course, no great weight in the balance of the body politic. But it smooths considerably the way for more serious influences, by giving the fictitious support of public clamour to the Jesuitical calculations of some crafty statesman, the promptings of fear, or the machinations of some influential military chief.

The Russia of to-day would be surely a very dangerous neighbourhood, and would have hardly limited herself to showing her teeth now and then, if there were nothing to moderate her ardour. But Russian masters have, so to speak, their legs confined in the stocks, which tighten in the same proportion as their desire to rush forward increases. The material decomposition, the financial difficulties, the disorder in all the branches of administration, including the army, exercise the most salutary and cooling effect even on those who govern Russia. The prospect of a defeat is not very well suited to restore the moral prestige of a party or a Government. Thus the longing for exploits abroad, and the fear lest the sword should be turned against its own breast, counterbalance each other. Which of these opposite, and equally peremptory, influences will prevail? In ordinary circumstances it is impossible to determine. Between this desire and this fear external circumstances must decide. Internal discontent, assuming a rather acute character, may drive the Russian Government to a desperate war at any price, as was the case with the third Napoleon. Any political difficulties in which the opposing countries may be involved, by diminishing the fear of them, may give the Russian Government greater inclination to pluck a fresh laurel at their expense. This is, of course, not particularly reassuring for the future, and few people are deceived on this point. But the real causes of the continual aggressive movement of the Russia of to-day do not lie here. Besides those accidental agencies, controllable, to a certain degree, by both parties, there is another of permanent activity, which merits our particular attention. My friend, Peter Kropotkin, has already pointed this out in his article in the *Nineteenth Century*, published under the title, "The Coming War;" it is the urgent necessity for obtaining access to foreign markets. But this is a tendency common to all modern industrial states, and in his brief notice Kropotkin deals in generalities, without mentioning how this common striving is manifested in Russia. This is what has induced me to take up this subject, and to try to connect with it some peculiarities of Russian life which may perhaps interest English readers.

II.

The Russian Autocracy is passing now through a very curious phase of its existence. Being based, as everywhere else in Europe, on the predominance of landowners and warriors, Russian Autocracy differed from western autocracies only in the fact that this latter class was composed of elements of somewhat different origin and character from those of other countries. But when the exigencies of social growth necessitated the emancipation of the serfs, Russia was remodelled at once after the pattern of its neighbouring states in everything but their political institutions. The form of government remained the same, but in social and economical life the middle class, the *bourgeoisie*, received as much predominance as in the rest of modern Europe. Moved by the tradition of the Autocracy as well as by the personal sympathies of those in power, the Government neglected nothing to maintain the former predominance of the landed gentry, and to atone for the material losses caused by the emancipation. First the land was deliberately over-estimated in value in all the provinces of Russia proper (excluding Poland, where the opposite course was adopted). Thus the annual payment for the redemption of land exacted from the peasants is also a monetary compensation for the loss of gratuitous labour. When, three years after the emancipation, the Zemstvos (local self-government) were created, the nobility received such a predominant power, that, if it chose to do so, the landed gentry could all at once transform the Zemstvos into so many oligarchies promoting and favouring the interest and privileges of the nobility. From the entering into office of Count Tolstoi, in 1866, the Government did its utmost to create a landed oligarchy mimicking English landlords, and at all times it has encouraged the nobility in their class selfishness and encroachment on the rights of the common weal, whilst obstructing every generous attempt to destroy the barriers of privilege. When shortly after the emancipation there appeared most unmistakable signs of the general ruin of the landed gentry, the Government proffered most liberal assistance. Hundreds of millions of roubles were showered on the nobility with reckless lavishness, to preserve this class from ruin. In 1867 the first territorial bank, with Government advances, was founded. In a few years their number grew to twelve. The total sum advanced to the nobles, both by the banks and by the State in the epoch of the emancipation, amounted to seven hundred millions of roubles. Besides which the landlords realised enormous sums by destroying and selling the greater part of their forests.

But all these rivers of gold were wasted, as water thrown on the sands of a desert. The ruin of the noblemen's estates was not prevented, and they were hardly benefited in any respect. The cultivation of the noblemen's land, if there is any cultivation at all, is in a most pitiable condition. They are overladen with debt, and their revenue is often nominal. Mr. Kaufmann's banking statistics show that in the whole agricultural region more than one-fourth of the soil is mortgaged to the territorial banks for large sums, which the landowners will never be able to pay. The only exceptions are the three provinces of the south-west, where, owing to some chance local peculiarity, the money was invested in productive improvements. As to the remainder of agricultural Russia, impartial statistics produce the following eloquent figures. In the provinces of the Lower Volga, the normal revenue, according to the valuation of the Zemstvos, being 116 kopecs for a *desiatine*, the interest for the debts contracted with the territorial banks takes 85 kopecs. The taxes, very moderate for the landlords' estates, amounting, in addition, to 11 kopecs from a *desiatine*, the proprietors receive only 20 kopecs from every *desiatine*. In the five provinces of the south (Black Sea region) the conditions are still worse. The average revenue, according to the valuation of the Zemstvos, being about 146 kopecs, the interest due to the banks amounts to 154 kopecs, which leaves a deficit of 22 kopecs, resulting in permanent failure to pay both the interest and the taxes. In the richest soil of the ten provinces of the black earth zone, where the net proceeds of a *desiatine* is 281 kopecs, the interest takes 228 kopecs, the taxes 15 kopecs, leaving for the proprietor only 38 kopecs per *desiatine*. The possibility of so enormous an absorption of income by interest is of course due to the overestimation of the land made by the too friendly agents of the territorial banks. And we must observe that the area of land thus irremediably involved in debt makes a very considerable part of the landlords' possessions. Only in the northern regions, where the land has hardly any value, is it not mortgaged. In the Black Sea zone, for example, the hypothecated land constitutes about 40 per cent. of the landlords' possessions; in the Lower Volga it approaches nearly 50 per cent., and there are provinces—for example, that of Kherson—where *all the land* held by landlords is in this condition. ("Annalles," 1880, N. 248.)

Nothing can be more damning than such figures. In this case bankruptcy, and the forced sale of the land by auction, is unavoidable. And they are really sold by dozens at every clearing up of the bank's accounts. But the condition of the estates of the bulk of the landed gentry is quickly approaching the same level. The careful statistical inquiries of the Moscow Zemstvo have startled all Russia, showing that in this province, possessing so enormous a market as the old capital, the estates of the landed gentry are in total ruin; the area of cultivated land is diminished to four-fifths, sometimes to one quarter of its former amount. In many districts there is no culture at all. The forests are wasted; even dairy farming, so profitable near the great towns, is in a most dejected state. Voices coming from all parts of the vast empire are repeating the same sad dirge. "The land yields nothing," is the general outcry of the nobility, and they rush from the country to the towns in quest of some employment in the State service or liberal professions, leaving the land either uncultivated, or abandoning it to the wasteful cultivation of cottiers, or selling it to new men,—some wealthy tavern keeper or former manager of serfs,—who are more fitted for the new mode of carrying on business in the villages.

It would cause a long digression to inquire into the agricultural condition created in Russia by the abstruse Emancipation Act, and to explain thoroughly why the landed gentry are going to ruin. The emancipation has ruined both the peasants and the landlords. The peasants have too little land to pay the exorbitant taxes, absorbing often the whole net proceeds of the soil. The landlords, on the other hand, can never secure a regular supply of agricultural labourers at the most important seasons, if they have not contrived to involve the surrounding peasantry in an inextricable network of debt. The peasants will not come at all, unless they are, however unwillingly, bound to work in the landlords' fields, leaving their own crops to perish in the meantime. The only thriving cultures are those based on this new sort of serfdom, to which the Russian peasant gave the name of *cabala;* the very same word which designated of old the act of selling one's self in slavery. There are very few exceptions to this rule. Now to organise and carry on for years such a system, a good many special qualities are required. A thorough intimacy with the surrounding rural population is the first requisite; but it is not enough. A good deal of cunning, pluck, and even cruelty and dishonesty are indispensable for ensnaring and binding the peasants in the most economical and effective way. The incapacity of our landed gentry for adapting themselves to our new agrarian condition is not, therefore, all to their dishonour. They have no pluck and little practical knowledge; but they most of them feel reluctant to play, with the help of the local police and the authorities, the part of peasant hunters, preferring to abandon their estates to their fate.

III.

However this may be, the nobility, as a landed class, is ruined, and is melting away because their property is really their only privilege. From a purely unproductive class of annuitants, formerly slave owners, the bulk of the Russian nobility is swelling continually another very interesting class of Russian society, on which we must dwell awhile. Most of the peculiarities of Russian life which surprise foreign observers are due to the existence and character of this class. It has no particular official designation or position, but it is engrossing almost entirely the most vital and most important of social functions, that of intellectual activity. In official documents these people, or rather a part of them, are designated under the generic name of *raznotchenzy*—literary men of variegated *chin*, or grade. The best equivalent for this incongruous term would be *intellectual proletariat*, which they really are. Their generic distinction is the possession of more or less superior mental culture of the European pattern, and the necessity of using it to earn their livelihood. In all countries people devoted to intellectual work as a profession are frequently destitute of other resources. But they form but a fraction of the vast number of men who, although belonging to the wealthy classes, do not neglect either study or various kinds of intellectual work as the means by which they may extend their political and social influence. Russia is a poor country compared with her western neighbours, and, owing to political conditions, there was no room for such aspirations. The literary career was the only one capable of tempting a nobleman, but the majority were too sluggish to take great interest in literary or scientific pursuits. All sorts of intellectual work was undertaken as a profession, and for no other reason. In the dawn of our culture this work was required by the State; later on there arose a considerable demand for it from the bulk of society and the nation. The intelligent worker could throw off the degrading official uniform, and serve his country no longer at the caprice of some high personage. But the general character of this class remained the same. It is the intellectual proletariat in the full acceptation of the term. We have only to cast a glance at the material condition of Russian high school students to feel it. The small nobility, having no land, or too little to live on, furnish a considerable contingent to this section; next comes the army of Government officials of the second and third order, who, by stinting themselves, can indeed give their children a sufficient education, but are unable to leave them a penny. A very considerable proportion is furnished at last by the priests of the Greek Church, whose numerous sons are frequently unwilling or unable to find room in the order.

These *raznotchenzy* furnish the bulk of the civil as well as the military officers of the Government, and manage all the branches of industry where some education is required. In science, literature, and all free professions they are the foremost. The emancipation of the serfs contributed largely to the extension of this class, both by diminishing the number of public drones and by causing a general diffusion of learning. And under the present political *régime* no class is suffering so greatly, and none is so deeply discontented. I will not dwell on the moral suffering caused by the total deprivation of the sacred human right to think and speak, which for intellectually developed men is simply stifling; this can easily be pictured. But what an English reader will surely fail to imagine are the continual petty vexations, obstructions, arbitrary interruptions and suppressions, which are constantly threatening all the unhappy Russians devoted to any branch of intellectual work. Be it the publication of a periodical paper or of a book, the foundation of an elementary school or of a co-operative association, the writers, publishers, teachers, promoters of any enterprise intended for something else than the plunder of the people, must suffer the oppression of the censorship, which is crippling their conceptions, and maiming their best ideas; while all the time there is no guarantee that their enterprise, and often their fortune also, will not be ruined by the brutal interference of some gendarme or police officer.

I will add that, of late, there are unmistakable signs that even such lame activity is becoming more and more difficult to obtain for men trained for intellectual work. A well-known Russian publicist, Mr. W. W., has collected in a recent paper many striking facts, showing that in all branches of professional work, medicine, superior teaching, agronomy, technology, in the last years is observable an overcrowding of applicants, showing a supply enormously surpassing the demand. Medicine, for example, which only a few years ago was regarded as the surest of bread-winning professions, is so full now, that for every place offered by the Zemstvos, or the municipalities, or the hospitals, and so forth, there is often a crowd of eighty to ninety applicants. Whilst formerly the Zemstvos had the greatest difficulty in obtaining a competent surgeon for the modest salary of about £120 to £150 a year, now they have only to pick out the best man from a crowd of bidders. There are instances when, profiting by the competition, some stingy Zemstvos have reduced their surgeon's salary from £130 to £90, or from £160 to £80 a year, and they could, if they wished, obtain them at still lower prices. High-class surgeons with scientific degrees are compelled to accept sometimes the office of simple phlebotomist at a salary of a few pounds a month. The Ministry of War, which had to spend so much money in scholarships in order to secure a staff of surgeons, because they preferred a free practice, now is so worried with aspirants that it must advertise to prevent surgeons from troubling them uselessly. And the official paper of the medical department now and then inserts emphatic appeals to public beneficence to support some graduated and experienced surgeons thrown on the street, and unable to find any employment whatever. In a word, the market is overloaded with the article so much sought for a few years ago. And yet nothing would be further from the truth than the supposition that the country has more medical men than it naturally requires. Russia has but one surgeon to every 6,400 inhabitants—one-fourth of the proportion in England, and one-tenth of that in the United States. But if we exclude the two capitals, which absorb one-fifth of the whole medical body, we shall have one surgeon to every 8,000 inhabitants. And still even in the provinces the towns take up the greatest and certainly the ablest part of the surgical staff. In the province of Kharkoff, for example, of the total number of 200 surgeons, 123 practise in the town of Kharkoff, and of the remaining 86 only 20 live in villages, the rest preferring to stay in the small towns of the province. Thus it happens that in the country parts of many provinces there is one surgeon for 47,000, for 50,000, and even for 73,000 of population. Official statistics show that on 100 people dead, 93 died without having been ever seen by any medical man. Only seven per cent. received some medical assistance. Such figures tell their own tale. The millions of Russian peasants remain without any surgical aid whatever, and the Zemstvos refuse to accept new surgeons offering their service, and reduce the miserable salary of those accepted. There is but one interpretation of this contradiction. Peasants are reduced to such misery that the Zemstvos cannot exact a kopec more from them. The cheapest medical assistance is for them an unattainable luxury. And the insignificant part of the town population which is sufficiently rich to afford it has enough and to spare with the handful of surgeons our medical schools can turn out. This state of things is repeated in all the most important professions. Russian agriculture is in the same state as it was in the thirteenth century, and of the 385 *agronomists* who studied in the Academy in the period of 1861-79, only thirty-six occupied in 1879 posts as managers on landlords' estates, and not one of them was engaged by the Zemstvos. In 1881, when, in the whole of Russia, the scourge of various epidemic diseases destroyed the peasants' cattle, the paper reported that more than one hundred veterinary surgeons were out of work, and had vainly applied for employment at the Ministry of the Interior, because the Zemstvos refused to engage them. (Poriadoc, 275.)

The position is quite clear. The acute crisis for the intellectual proletariat has begun. The bulk of this class has already, or soon will be, thrown on the street, because the peasant, the only employer requiring their services, is totally ruined. The close union of interests between the brain worker and the operative was always strongly felt by the most enlightened Russians. Among our best writers, publicists, critics, poets, novelists,—the teachers of the nation in general,—this feeling, enlightened by humanitarian Western philosophy, was fruitful of the best consequences. Notwithstanding the severity of the censorship, they always contrived to give it shape in the literature by which the three last generations were educated. The generous Democracy developed in all Russian educated classes, beginning with the *raznotchenzy* and lower nobility, and diminishing as it approached the higher orders—this Democracy is most promising for our future. It will never be rooted out or crushed by the efforts of the Government, and will always animate our best men in their struggle against the Autocracy for the sake of their own and the peasants' freedom. Now it asserts itself, as we have seen, in the most peremptory way. It speaks not only to the heads or hearts of the people, but to their stomachs— a part of the body which in many is the most sensible to persuasion. Even the officials of the Government, save the few superior ones, must feel uneasy, if not for themselves, at all events for their children, if they care about their future.

Thus the mass of intelligent and educated Russians grow more and more unanimous in their discontent against the existing order of things. The removal of the present political *régime*, which is the cause of the misery of the nation, is a question of life and death for our intellectual class. It appeals to everything which can be appealed to. This accounts for the tenacity of the revolution, which no bloody reprisal can extirpate, and also for the large sympathy it meets with amongst all classes. And that is also what makes the position of the Government a very dangerous one. It cannot sweep out these deadly enemies, because a modern state cannot live a day without making use of a vast amount of intellectual power. But can a Russian student, nourished by our noble, humanitarian literature, can he don the livery of a Tzar's servant, and become one of the blood-suckers of the peasants? Certainly not. A Siberian convict's grey overcoat will oppress his shoulders much less than the uniform of an official. Only the morally destitute, the cynically egotistical, the renegades of their better selves, can deliberately accept the position of the Tzar's *tchinovniks*. Hence the dishonesty, plunder, malversation for which the Tzar's administration has become notorious. And as to the many who enter the official body from necessity or from traditional habit, they become either wretchedly discontented, or take to plotting against the Government. The unbiassed testimony of the secret memorandum of Count Schouvaloff, formerly head of the Third Section, and Ambassador to England, shows that the general disaffection of the main body of *tchinovniks* is not a secret from the Government. And the no less unbiassed testimony of the list of the political arrests shows that affiliation to revolution is as common among the officials as among the other classes of society. A very dangerous position it is for a Government to have to lean on such a staff of people, charged with ill omens, affording a particularly favourable ground for conspiracies of every kind, from the small one manifested in acts of terrorism to the large one, the violent *coup d'état*, which sooner or later will overthrow the Autocracy and the Autocrats, if the general decomposition of the State does not force the Government to lay down its arms.

IV.

But what are the chances of the Government? For it must have, after all, some support to uphold it, otherwise, rotten as it is, it could not stand against the four winds of heaven. It is in the agricultural masses that the existing *régime* finds its chief support,—not so much on account of their devotion, which is rather a sort of superstition, as on account of their patience. The masses supply the soldiers for a colossal army, and obediently pay the taxes, making an enormous total revenue. By unscrupulous use of force and money, by corrupting one and slaughtering another, much can be done; not all, however. Even a conqueror who has imposed his yoke on a country by force of arms, if he is provident, will always try to conciliate the good graces of some large part of the body social. It would seem at first sight that, for Russian Autocracy, the fittest class on which to make such an attempt would be the peasantry. For nothing seems easier than to convert, by some real benefits, what now is a simple misunderstanding into true attachment. And, indeed, the Government of Alexander III., who professes to be a peasants' Tzar, tried in the years 1881-3, with great pomp and roll of drums, some petty experiments in democratic Cæsarism. But it failed miserably, without being able to improve in the least degree the desperate economical condition of the peasants. For to benefit the masses is a task far beyond the resources, both material and intellectual, of a bureaucratic despotism. All that the latter is able to do, without renouncing its uncontrolled power, is to give a share of the booty to some clique it wishes to gain over. But whom can it choose for its accomplices and allies? That is the question. The landed gentry are useless; the professional and educated classes hopeless. But, lo! there is the middle-class man, standing on the lookout, and eagerly awaiting an opportunity of making himself serviceable. His former existence was a most wretched one, and his position dependent and often humiliating in the extreme. The nobles were really screening the sunlight from him. Having the exclusive right of owning serfs, they excluded him from the possession of the chief wealth of the country,—the land,—which had no value without a labouring force to cultivate it. They occupied all posts of honour; they were pre-eminent everywhere. The national industry was in quite a rudimentary state, lacking the chief requisite for its development,—the free workmen,—because the serfs, when the nobles or the Crown graciously permitted them to abandon the furrow, were the chief recruits for our industrial establishments. Besides, there was but a very limited demand for the productions of regular manufactories. The peasants provided for most of their needs by home industry, the women of the households weaving linen and rough woollen stuffs for the hawkers. The iron and leather wares, and other goods which could not be produced by home labour, were supplied for the whole country by the so-called *custary*—a kind of home-working artisan, half agriculturalist, scattered over the surface of Russia in hamlets and villages, having each its hereditary and special branch of industry. The landowners, having at their disposal vast territorial possessions, and forty millions of slaves to till them, had enormous masses of agricultural produce for sale and exportation, and were the richest consumers. But their capricious and high-class demands could be satisfied most advantageously by foreign importation.

Thus the greatly predominant typical middle-class man of the epoch anterior to the emancipation was almost exclusively a merchant. And so this class was officially designated in Russia. Now this particular occupation may require a good deal of cunning and practical ability, but it demands little, if any, of the scientific knowledge which manufacturing industries do. The Russian merchants of the old type, as regards their intellectual development, differed little from the peasants. The bulk of them were illiterate; and even in our time the notables of the merchant class in provincial towns, members of municipal councils, often can hardly decipher the title of a newspaper, and in writing never commit themselves further than in scrawling their names. The fact being that, when Peter the Great by Herculean impulse tried to elevate the Russian nation from Muscovite stagnation to Western culture, only the head of the social body, seized by the hair, followed the violent pull. The body remained behind. The nation was split in two, and the merchant class remained on the other side, with the peasants keeping their old customs and their old uncontaminated ignorance. They suffered many annoyances for the sake of their long beards and old Russian dress, and the majority of them adhered to the schism of the ritualistic old orthodoxy, shunning with sacred horror the culture borrowed from foreign heretics.

The two most influential classes of the nation—the nobility and the merchants—preserved all the antagonism and exclusiveness of two castes, differing by birth, habits, and traditions. The nobles mocked the merchants for their gross ignorance, and despised them for their moral character. For in Russia of old, as in all barbarous countries, cheating and fraud were considered the fundamental principles of a thriving commerce. " No cheating, no selling," is the proverb of the Russian tradespeople, and all observers agree, that even in our time commercial honesty is not a virtue in which Russian merchants excel. It would be gross partiality to say that the Russian nobility were very strict in the matter of the eighth commandment. But, somewhat like the Germans described by Tacitus, they were ashamed to steal by fraud what they could rob quite frankly as their due as State officials, administrators, and dispensers of justice. The counting-house people were in very bad odour with the nobility, and to allow a merchant to sit at one's dining table was considered an act of supreme condescension.

The merchants, on the other hand, repaid the nobles with similar ill-feeling, despising and ridiculing their indolence, incapacity for business, and reckless profligacy. They valued not a straw the superior culture and various intellectual accomplishments of those French-speaking, elegant gentlemen. In the eyes of a genuine merchant every nobleman was but a helpless fool, whom clever people, like himself, were in duty bound to cheat and deceive. The plucky and unscrupulous merchant had, however, to conceal in the depths of his soul the sentiment of his own superiority; because in all strife with him it was the nobles who held the knife by the handle. Administration, justice, police—all was in those times subject, directly or indirectly, to the nobles; and for a person belonging to an inferior class it was a hopeless, often a perilous, enterprise to take an action against any member of the privileged order. "A raven will not pick out another raven's eye," say the Russian people. The merchant was at the mercy of the barbarous whim of every wild nobleman, whom the habit of living among slaves had not taught to respect human dignity. Only by making a show of craven obsequiousness and hypocritical reverence could a merchant coming to transact business with a country gentleman preserve himself from the worst treatment and even personal assaults.

In the towns, the centres of civilisation, the merchant was more or less saved from having a couple of dogs set at his heels, or his beard burnt or any similar practical joke, by the proximity of the police, with whom he was generally on friendly terms. But his position was a most wretched one nevertheless. For he was exposed, bound hand and foot, to the petty tyranny of local authorities. True, their relation bore the stamp of rough familiarity, after a Russian fashion, and even they were sometimes allies, indispensable to each other. "Oh, you rogues, scoundrels, arch-knaves, seven devils and one witch in your throats! you wanted to ruin me by complaining to His Excellency!" shouts the most typical of our Superintendents of police, the hero of Gogol's "Revizor," addressing the penitent merchants standing before him. "Have you forgotten, ungrateful dogs that you are, how many times I have helped you to cheat the Government? Was it not I who assisted you, miscreant swindlers, to palm off on the Crown Commission your worthless, rotten rubbish?" And the contrite delinquents can but plead guilty, protesting that it was the devil that seduced them to complain against so fatherly a master, and they are pardoned on condition of bringing a new bribe. To bribe always, to bribe every member of the official hierarchy "according to their rank," and to be worried, harassed, threatened in order to further extortions—such was the fate of our middle-class men in times not long gone by. Like the Jew of the Middle Ages, the merchant had to conceal his riches in order not to provoke cupidity, and having his strong box brimful of silver and gold, he lived like a beggar, eating nothing but sour cabbages with bread, lest his opulence might cause the doubling of his bribe.

He was a very poor figure, our middle-class man before 1861. But the emancipation came, giving all at once a new aspect to the country. With the abolition of serfdom the nobility practically lost the character of a privileged class. The chief source of the national wealth—the land—could be henceforward acquired by everybody, since its possession did not imply slave ownership. Vast tracts of land, making in all about one-fourth of the noblemen's possessions, have already passed from the hands of the ruined nobles into those of the merchants and new men of their stamp; another fourth being mortgaged to the banks, of which they are the shareholders, is in their virtual possession. The millions of peasants, who formerly worked for the nobles, now are enriching with their labour the merchants, who found excellent means of adapting themselves to new agrarian conditions. Swarms of peasants, compelled by hunger, and no longer detained by anybody's will, are rushing to the towns, and crowd at the doors of the manufactories, imploring work for the lowest wages. After the emancipation all the country began to move. New means of com munication were required to suit this new life, and in a few years Russia was covered with a network of railways. National industry received a wonderful push. It has quintupled in the last twenty years. (Elisée's "Russian Geography.") Commercial and industrial enterprises of every kind, banks, companies of every description, sprang up like mushrooms after a rainy day. The country entered with the extreme rashness characteristic of all our social process upon an entirely new phase of its existence. And the hero of it is he, the formerly despised, insulted, creeping merchant. He is everywhere: as a landowner, elector of the provincial assembly, as capitalist and rich tradesman, he reigns in the municipalities. He alone is prosperous, and the ruined nobles now accept with gratitude lucrative employment in his office. He is quite at ease now. From a milch cow, whom only the lazy abstained from milking, he became the most respectable and courted member of the community. He is no longer afraid of the menials of administration, who are now at his beck, anxious to earn as a gratuity what formerly they took by force. The abolition of slavery has cleared social life from many a pestilent emanation of private tyranny, and new tribunals, with jurymen and publicity of procedure, judging all people, all offences (except, of course, anything political), are prompt to redress any injury, especially to a man who can secure the services of the very best counsel.

But all this prosperity showered on him could not change him personally. True, his former mean-ness, timidity, and obsequiousness has been quickly turned into presumption and insolence toward his inferiors, whom he can trample down. For towards the big people he becomes all at once mean and slavish. He has learned to spend lavishly, and to make a show of his wealth, because now it can only increase his reputation and influence. To make himself more acceptable to the circles where he is so kindly received, he has thrown off his old-fashioned *kaftan* and donned the European overcoat; sometimes shaving off his sacred beard. But he has not in the least become an European. He is utterly ignorant, and has none of those intellectual needs which culture has generated in his European *confrère*. The middle class—the *bourgeoisie*—of European countries is a class uniting in itself the greatest forces which modern culture possesses, wealth and culture—being not only the richest, but the most enlightened class of the nation. That is what urged it to rise in arms against despotism and gave it at the same time the force to subdue the Monarchy and the territorial aristocracy. In Russia, as we have seen, the genuine middle-class men possess only one, and that not the most important of these two qualifications—wealth, coupled with great denseness of brain; whilst the intellectual power belongs to another class, which possess none of the force and influence over the masses which wealth gives. This most unfortunate and anomalous division cannot last long. Out of the 10,000 students in our universities, about 3,800 belong to the middle class, which in old times was hardly represented at all in our high schools. As to gymnasia (colleges), the pupils belonging to the non-privileged classes form at present the majority. The middle class is growing more and more educated, in defiance of relentless and most cynical obstruction on the part of the so-called Ministry of Public Education. But until now the division between wealth and intellect has been strongly marked, and the Government well knows how to make the best of it. The newly-born *bourgeoisie*, composed of merchants, enriched burghers, country usurers, and tavern keepers, are really the best, the surest, the only sincere supporters of the existing *régime;* because they are siding not with the imaginary, mythical Tzar, as the peasants are, but with the real one, the head and informing soul of the existing state, with its oppression, arbitrariness, peculation, and cruelties. For all the wrongdoing of the Autocratic system does not affect our new *bourgeois* in the least. How can he feel the suppression of liberty of speech when he has nothing to say? or of the liberty of the press, when he reads nothing but the advertisements? He is too narrow-minded as yet to conceive the idea that a better political order, by improving the general condition of the country, will increase tenfold the income of all his class. He finds it much more advantageous to turn to his private benefit the prevailing arbitrariness and venality, which put at his service for a miserable bribe the political forces of the State.

Thus both the parties are in perfect harmony. The Government, which cares about nothing but its own existence, is quite happy in having found such supporters and allies, and the game goes on merrily. The purest of middle-class *régimes*, with a *bourgeois* king of the stamp of a Louis Philippe, could not sacrifice with half such selfishness the interests of the whole nation to those of the *bourgeoisie* as did the Tzars Alexander II. and III. Nobody has calculated yet the total amount of funds spent in direct subsidies to various industrial, railway, and steamboat companies, as well as to private manufacturers of every description, " in order to support the national industry." But judging by what was published, as regards the railway, for example, we must conclude that it exceeded five or six times what was wasted on the nobility. It is to be reckoned by milliards of roubles—like the contributions imposed on a defeated country. Selfish as they are, our capitalists want nevertheless to shun any contribution to the Exchequer of the State which is benefiting them with such liberality. When the Zemstvos, in the years 1865-6, passed a resolution to tax the capital employed in industry, the capitalists prevailed upon the Government to issue a special law (19th November, 1867), expressly prohibiting the taxation of the revenue of the industrial concerns. Thus was maintained a very onerous and unjust exemption in favour of the richest citizens.

With other classes, the nobility included, the Government show always a certain diffidence. In instituting the Zemstvos, and giving them entirely into the hands of the nobility, the Government take care to exclude the small nobility, by establishing a high qualification for the suffrage. With the middle-class men the Autocracy is much more confident. The municipal statute of 1870, conferring a certain amount of municipal self-government, leaves our towns completely at the mercy of those middle-class men. It excludes the main body of the educated class, but none of those who are educated by the doubtful morality of our counting-houses. The ignorant shop assistants and errand boys paying for their commercial licenses four or five shillings a year, have a vote for the election of municipal councillors, whilst the citizens who do not belong to any trade, but are members of respectable free professions, — professors at universities, surgeons, lawyers, etc.,—have no right to vote unless they are freeholders of houses, which, being very exceptional in Russia, virtually excludes the most enlightened class of Russian society from any voice in the management of the towns in which they live. When this system bore its fruit, and a series of scandalous bankruptcies of municipal banks exhibited such a corruption in the municipalities as equalled (unable to surpass) everything previously known about bureaucratic malversations, there was a general outcry throughout the country, that something must be done to stop the impudent embezzlement of the public money. The extension of the municipal franchise to the instructed classes was demanded,— a very modest demand,—as the simplest means of checking the cynical dishonesty of our respectable town notables. But the Government remained deaf to this clamour; it thought it quite a sufficient guarantee to prohibit near relations from becoming managers of the same banks.

Protection of trade was always eagerly desired by our middle class. At every chilling draught from the Berlin, Paris, and London markets, unable to protect themselves, they whimpered for protective tariffs, and the Government hastened to the rescue of its cherished children. The customs duties being continually augmented, converted the protective tariff into a prohibitory one, closing entirely the Russian markets to foreign, especially to German, imports.

The Moscow manufacturer hoped to sleep undisturbed in the shadow of the *Moscow Gazette*. But here a very curious event took place, which marred his prospects. The German products could not cross the frontier, but nothing could prevent the German producers from doing so in a body. Unable to send their wares to Muscovy, the German manufacturers, with their capital, workmen, and machinery, crossed the Russian frontier, and pitched their tents on the other side of it. They chose for settlement Poland, as a country better known to them and more fitting to their tastes. The district of Lodz became the centre of German colonisation. Formerly a small village, Lodz is now the second city of Poland by its population and by its industry. Seven-eights of all the cotton wares of Poland are manufactured in this town. The cotton-wool and dyeing manufactories—most of them German—extend for a distance of more than ten kilometres. The same is true with respect to neighbouring towns. All the district is at present more German than Polish.

Thus the dreaded enemy entered the walls, and hurled their packages of wares against their adversaries. This was a most unexpected and untoward occurrence for the Russian manufacturer. The products of German textile manufactories found an excellent and always increasing market in Russia.

They are now beginning to obtain a footing in the old capital itself. It was a great disappointment and a great annoyance to our long-bearded Muscovites; but the Paladin of all the swindling and pilfering legion, the editor of the *Moscow Gazette*, was equal to the occasion, and began a fiery literary campaign, advocating the establishment of an *interior frontier*, cutting out Poland from the Russian markets, by imposing custom duties on goods of Polish manufacture. That would be a very energetic measure indeed, and a very amusing one also. For, suppose the project of Mr. Katkoff realised, what would prevent the Germans from crossing the new interior frontier? What is to be done if they come to Moscow at one stride?

But in June 1885 the editor of the *Moscow Gazette* has gone still farther. He proposed nothing less than to sell *Poland* to *Germany* for some million of roubles, to free the Moscow manufacturers at once from this dangerous competitor. This is certainly the height of absurdity; but what can be more characteristic than to hear such an opinion expressed by a man who is by no means a simple journalist, whose whims have no importance? Mr. Katkoff is something like a permanent cabinet minister without portfolio, one of the three men who rule the ruler of the Russian Empire.

v.

It is impossible to go farther, and it is difficult to go so far. No statesman, no leading political paper in a country where the middle class reigns supreme, would have seriously proposed such an absurdity as selling an integral part of the State—officially recognised as such, at all events—to another power, because its industry is too much in advance of that of the other provinces. No Government, representing the interest of the middle class, would impose permanent contributions in favour of a small set of private men, nor maintain an onerous immunity from taxes in favour of those who are most capable of supporting the burden of State expenses. All this is impossible in a middle-class state, because contrary to the interests of this class itself as a body. But a despotic government is no more capable of furthering the interests of the middle class than those of the masses of the people; because the middle class, as a whole, requires for its prosperity, in the first instance, general liberty, self-government, the better management of public funds, and public control over the officials. The Russia of to-day, as a state, is nothing but a bureaucratic oligarchy, serving with slavish devotedness a commercial oligarchy of the worst kind.

An altogether peculiar position for an Autocracy.

Now having by the whole of its proceedings ruined the country and reduced the peasants, who form nine-tenths of the nation, to a state of virtual starvation, which excludes them wholesale from the chance of becoming buyers, the Government must make shift to answer the desperate cry of these people about the absence of any outlet for their produce. The only expedient which is open to the Government is to acquire new external markets. Having all the western markets shut off, and being unable to compete with foreign producers even in

Asiatic markets, it tries to supplement, by force of arms, the deficiency of industrial skill.

This is the chief reason why Russia is a conquering country; military ambition is only secondary. It is suggestive to look at Professor Arminius Vambéry's map of Russian advances in Central Asia, the enormous area of land, surpassing Austria and Germany put together, representing Russian acquisitions in the last one hundred and fifty years, about two-fifths of which was conquered in the brief period following 1863; *i.e.*, in the commercial phase of the Russian State. This gives a rate of advance for the new epoch four and a half times quicker than that of the old military period.

But all the support the Moscow industry can have from the opening of the Central Asian markets, such as the Khanates, Penjdeh, and even Herat, is very limited. Russia must profit by every opportunity of advancing further its line of Cossacks and custom houses, in order to send under their protection bales of wares.

Where will this march stop? That is a question which particularly interests the English. Is it likely that the Russian battalions will disturb them on the other side of the Indus? Does the Russian Government really cherish hostile plans against the Indian Empire? Such questions are continually asked in this country, and we must answer them to the best of our ability. Many eminent writers and politicians have tried to do so, but all in vain, since the question is not advanced a step, and hardly admits at all of a distinct answer. Professor Arminius Vambéry and some other writers think otherwise. Accepting as evidence the geographical fact, that the new acquisitions advance the Russian frontier to India, they conclude that there is a premeditated, a well-determined design on the part of the Russian Tzars. That such a dream may cross now and then some fantastic mind amongst our St. Petersburg rulers is very probable. But I think it would be doing our Government too much honour to attribute to it any strongly determined and firmly continued line of conduct in any matter whatever. We Russians, witnessing the daily policy of the Government in internal questions, know that there was hardly one in which the Government has not contradicted itself many times in the course of a few years—from the greatest questions, as the emancipation of the peasants, the Zemstvos, the press —down to secondary ones, as the Jewish question. Everywhere we see the same uncertainty, vacillation, repeated contradictions, absence of any determined plan. And this chaos increases rather than subsides with the times. Even so moderate a writer as Mr. A. Leroy Beaulieu, in speaking of Russian home politics during the last epoch, says: "The last years of the period following the emancipation have been in every respect a period of confusion, reaction, and retreat. Hardly any Government has ever shown such indecision, and such contradiction to its own views, knowing neither how to conclude what it had begun, nor to destroy what it had initiated;"* and the monarchist and slavophil

---

* " Les dernières années de l'emancipation ont été a tout égard une période de confusion, de réaction, et de recul ; jamais peut-être un gouvernment ne s'est montré aussi irresolu, aussi en

Kosheleff, who was personally acquainted with the members of the St. Petersburg cabinet, says that all the ministers of the Tzar live from hand to mouth, thinking only how they can get through the day, and not knowing in the evening what they are going to do to-morrow.

Is it possible that such a Government is capable of the constancy and steadiness of purpose ascribed to it as regards its foreign policy? It is more than doubtful. The people ruling in both departments being the same, in both branches the same principle, or rather absence of principle, prevails, and in foreign policy the Government follows the impulse of external events and influences of the moment, without any decided plan for the future. Thus it is rather pushed from behind, than rushing headlong after some long-determined purpose. For the present an immediate campaign against India is an absurdity. But the nearer the frontier approaches the easier will it be. And the French say "*l'appetit vient en mangeant.*" The great check to the satisfaction of this appetite is, however, to be remembered: the present forces of the Russian Colossus are greatly exaggerated in Europe, notwithstanding the many tests of it. Russian finances are quickly approaching those of Turkey. Its army is numerous and excellent so far as the *personnel* is concerned. But it is gnawed by the gangrene of official peculation, which works more ravages in its ranks than any enemy with whom it has had to cope. In such

désaccord avec lui-même, ne sachant ni achever ce qu'il avait commencé, ni détruire ce qu'il avait ébauché." (*Revue des Deux Mondes*, 1882.)

conditions a war to be carried on in a country distant many thousands of miles from the centres of population, and certain to be protracted for a long time, is particularly dangerous. I will not play the alarmist. My object is simply to expose both sides of the question, leaving my readers to draw their own inferences. For myself, I will suggest only one, with which most of my readers will agree, I hope—that the surest and simplest way to solve all doubt and to remove all uncertainty would be the destruction of the Autocracy.

CHAPTER IV.

THE POLITICAL FORM OF THE RUSSIA OF THE FUTURE.

WELL, the reader will say to the last words of the preceding chapter, the Autocracy must be destroyed. But is revolution really so certain a guarantee against foreign aggression ? Who knows whether the chronic danger Russian despotism presents will not manifest itself at the outbreak of a revolution by a wild rush for external conquests? Was it not so in France? Will not history be repeated in Russia also ?

No Russian, unless he has spent all his lifetime abroad, will entertain such doubts and apprehensions. But they exist, to a certain degree, in the minds of the English. I will, therefore, ask permission to dwell for a moment upon facts, which, if not unknown, are at all events not sufficiently taken into consideration; otherwise the misapprehensions about our future would have been impossible. I refer to the absence of any tendency to centralisation in the Russian nation itself.

The unification of France, ethical, intellectual, and political,—due to the high standard of French civilisation radiating from Paris,—was an accomplished fact long before the Revolution. When this latter broke out none but a strongly centralised government was possible in France. During the unexampled social fermentation of that period the provinces showed no inclination for autonomy and local independence. The innocent dreams of federalism of the unfortunate Girondists were considered as treason, and among the imaginary crimes imputed to them one of the heaviest was that of desiring the "dismembering of France." And notwithstanding the numerous changes of her political constitution and great progress in her political liberties, the centralised form of government remained unshaken, the first practical manifestation of federalism being made by the so much calumniated Commune of 1871.

Now the centralisation of political power in any shape,—be it in the form of the Roman senate or of the French Committee of Safety,— if not necessarily aggressive, is always liable to be hurried into foreign war. France, moreover, was enticed into it by external aggression. The usurpation of Napoleon I. was the consequence both of this centralisation and of those wars, and he only pushed to an extreme what had preceded him.

The social conditions of Russia are quite the reverse of those of France. Only the central ethnical nucleus of the Russian Empire—Muscovy proper—was formed by a natural process of unification, having some analogy to that of France; the remnant being either conquered by main force or annexed voluntarily, to be enchained the following day. None of these elements were ever fused in the ruling nationality; Muscovite habits had no attractiveness, and their culture was often much lower than that of the annexed country. Whilst the German inhabitants of Alsace and Lorraine, conquered by the French, became, after a few generations, most ardent French patriots, the Ruthenian population, for example, formerly a military republic, and annexed in 1654 by the decision of its popular assembly, is not assimilated with Russia proper after two centuries of common life. Excluding the handful of nobles and the official classes, the Ruthenians speak their own language, have their own national customs, and, I venture to add, their own religion, genuine Greek orthodoxy; whilst the real worship of the peasants of great Russia is sectarianism. The Ruthenian peasants do not remember the early history of their republican institutions, but they feel strongly that their national individuality is distinct from the dominant great Russian nation, to which they still give the old name of *Moskals*—*i.e.*, Muscovites. Even among the superior and educated classes of the towns, we observe during the last two generations a strong revival of national feeling under the influence of the democratic ideas of our time. So it is with the people who are, by blood, by religion, by language, the nearest of kin to the Russians. I need hardly speak of other nationalities—Poles, Lithuanians, Finns, Caucasians, and many others—under the dominion of the Tzar by the force of the bayonet, and separated from the dominant nationality by religion, language, and old historical traditions, with nothing to atone for the loss of their national freedom and to reconcile them to their rulers. Modern Russia possesses no absorbent power.

Such various elements are not likely to crave the maintenance of the centralised form of government, when once they are free to have their own way.

Nor is that all. Even in the genuine Russian provinces there is no trace of centralistic tendencies. The long centuries of bureaucratic despotism, to which the enormous distances gave unlimited sway, produced such a universal aversion to centralisation, that in this respect there is hardly any difference between the genuine Russian and the leading men of other nationalities. Nobody but the bureaucratic officials of the Government are partisans of centralisation. Even the obtuse Muscovite slavophiles, like M. Axakoff, representing extreme Russian conservatism, akin in sympathy to the upholders of the official status, desire a large development of local self-government as the sole guarantee against bureaucratic tyranny.

Under such conditions there is no possibility of maintaining a centralised empire. Whether the present *régime* shall be destroyed by an insurrection,—which is certainly the speediest and the least painful way of getting rid of it,—or whether, in consequence of a long and morbid process of internal decomposition and of the impending national bankruptcy, the Government will be obliged to appeal to the country, as was the case in France, the result will be the same. Russia, as soon as she obtains the faculty of adjusting herself according to her own disposition, will cease to be a centralised empire. And we may add that the greater the liberty enjoyed at this reconstruction, the fewer will be the centralised elements which will remain in it.

POLITICAL FORM OF THE RUSSIA OF THE FUTURE. 87

There are, however, strong reasons for inferring that this interior segregation will never arrive at a total dismemberment of the State. I do not refer to Finland, the Caucasus, or the Central Asian conquests, quite heterogeneous elements, which have nothing to do with Russia, and are rather an encumbrance to a free state. They will certainly fall off and constitute themselves into independent States, or perhaps unite with the neighbouring countries. With them the Russian people have nothing to do. What is worth consideration is the political attitude of the formerly independent states of Sclav origin occupying the great eastern plain. To get a clue to it we must dwell for a moment on the condition of Poland. If there is a country which may reasonably be expected to adhere to the idea of an entire secession, it is undoubtedly Poland. No country has suffered so much from Russian despotism, and in no one is the national sentiment so keen. Nevertheless, it is highly improbable that, should a favourable change in Russian political conditions take place, even Poland would secede. The reason is as simple as it is conclusive. In our times of great manufacturing industries and coming social changes, economical considerations weigh enormously in the political balance. Now, from our remarks on the relations of Polish and Russian industry, with which the reader is familiar from a former chapter, it is evident that even at the present time, in the miserable condition of the Russian nation, the union with this country presents considerable economical advantages to Poland. This small country stands now at the head of our industries, which afford it a vast, we may say an unbounded, market for its products. A wise nation will think twice before forsaking this advantage for the mere pleasure of having a king or a president of its own. And the perfect mutual understanding between the most advanced political parties of both countries indicates that the time is close at hand when the old barrier of hatred dividing both nations will give place to a better feeling.

But no amount of freedom of export, nor even general liberty and security, will reconcile the Poles to union with Russia if they do not obtain a complete assertion of their nationality. They will demand Home Rule; because if they have to send their deputies to a common central parliament, they will be swamped by the mass of deputies representing the millions of other nationalities. For, according to their present numbers, they would only be one twenty-fifth part of the whole body. It would only be a new kind of subjection for them.

The Polish question is only an extreme case amongst many others. The Ruthenian is a reproduction in a more moderate form of the Polish problem. Here the secession would be not disadvantageous, but simply impossible, since the provinces occupying the middle part of the rivers forming the natural line of communication cannot secede from the provinces holding their sources and mouths. And, indeed, there is no political party in this country nourishing the idea of secession.

But mere separation into nationalities cannot satisfy the desire for liberty in so enormous a State as Russia. For we must remember that the homogeneous Ruthenians number about seventeen millions, and occupy an area equal to that of France. Great Russia numbers forty millions, a population equal to that of the German Empire, and scattered over a much greater area. Constituted as single states according to nationalities, they would still make enormous centralised bureaucratic states, with no real self-government and with the additional draw back of possible interior struggles. Further subdivision will necessarily be called for. My friend, Professor Michel Dragomanoff, the leader of the Ruthenian Radical movement, thinks that his country must be divided into no less than three independent parts. For great Russia, taking into account its size, the number of subdivisions must be at least three times greater. This is, of course, the best guarantee against the possibility of national rivalry, and at the same time the sole mode of obtaining that unification of the State which is desirable for the purpose of national defence, combined with the great variety of differences of the diverse tribes and nations living on the vast eastern plain, and the traditional habit of self-government in which the Russian peasantry is educated by the self-governing village communes.

Thus the only form into which Russia, when once free, can mould itself, will be a series of autonomous states, each having Home Rule—that is, legislative and executive power, with a central government providing for the general interest of the whole union; a form of government of which the United States of America furnishes us with an example. This is not a political dream or theoretical desideratum; it is the simple inference drawn from the natural condition of our country, the ultimate and inevitable end of our political evolution. How soon this final form is likely to be attained; whether the remoulding of the Russian State will be done at once or by a gradual process of compromise with the existing monarchical institutions, is, of course, another question, which only the future can answer. But it is beyond doubt that every change will bring the country nearer to this ultimate form. It is not at all impossible for the Monarchy to come to an agreement with the nation. To people laying so much stress on social amelioration as all Russian advanced parties do, the mere form of a Republic—though preferable, of course—does not present the same fascination as to the French Montagnard of 1793, or the Italian patriots of Mazzinian persuasion. General civil rights and political freedom have always been placed foremost by the advanced parties of Russia, and the example of England shows that these are not incompatible with a Monarchy. Russia would willingly have abstained from shedding blood for the mere chance of giving a better sounding name to the chief of the State, provided, of course, that the standing army be substituted by a national militia. But in discussing the chances of any compromise the dispositions of both contending parties are to be taken into account. Practically the Russian movement for freedom has to deal with the most stubborn dynasty the world has ever seen, and which has always shown a most desperate incapacity for understanding the interests both of the nation and itself. To hope for the conversion of the Romanoffs to a true liberal policy, is indeed to be a dreamer of the most incorrigible nature. It is more than probable that, as the struggle advances, Russian patriots will openly inscribe the word "Republic" on their banner. And even a court revolution will be hopeless unless it exalt to the throne some junior branch less imbued with traditional short-sighted despotism, and less insensible to reason than the elder one.

However it may be, one thing is certain—every step Russia makes towards liberty will diminish the danger of its military encroachment. And the more the interior transmutation is radical, the surer such a result becomes. Nothing can be so incorrect as the supposition that a Russian revolution may result in the outburst of warlike propensities. There is no such feeling in the Russian people. The urgent necessity for protecting the soil against the incessant invasions of Asiatic nomads, to whom the country was open from every part, turned Russia into a centralised despotic State. And when there were no longer any invasions, the Autocracy continued the expansion of the empire on its own behalf. But the character of the race proved stronger than the combined efforts of the past and the present Russian rulers. By a strange contradiction the most aggressive of European nations is really the most pacific in its disposition. Richard Cobden said of them: "The Russians are, perhaps, naturally the least warlike people in the world. All their tastes and propensities are of an opposite character. Even in their amusements there is an absence of rudeness and violence" (Cobden's

"Political Writings," p. 273); and he corroborates his statement by quoting Mr. Danby Seymour, who was rather distrustful of Russia as a political power, but has the impartiality to testify that "the most singular thing is that the people among whom this military organisation prevails is, without exception, the most pacific nation on the face of the earth ; and upon this point, I believe, no difference of opinion exists among all observers. Having lived for several years in a position which enabled me to mix much with the officers and men of the Russian army, such is my strong conviction of the Russian character." Mr. Hathausen mentions as a point, admitting, no doubt, the absence of all warlike tendency among the Russian people: "The Russian people have no pleasure in wearing arms like the Turks or the Poles ; and the duel which now often takes place among Russian officers is contrary to the national manners, and a custom imported from the West."

With such a disposition of its people, a free Russia, with its political arrangements so constituted as to be particularly unfavourable to any adventurous foreign policy, prosperous and enlightened because free, Russia will for ever cease to be a threat to European tranquillity. Having so many interior wants to satisfy, and so many important questions to solve at home, it will certainly become the sure guarantee of peace. Let us only observe that having now a population of a little more than one hundred millions, in the space of sixty-four years this number will be doubled, according to Elisée Reclus' ("Geography") average rate of multiplication of the Russian people. With its present population Russia could afford to have an army of about four millions of men, but that the finances of the States will not bear the incorporation of such a mass in the ranks of the standing army; and the despotic form of government prevents the institution of a territorial militia. I abstain from computing to what number such a militia might attain in a few score years. Russia is the only country which requires no standing army to withstand even the strongest military powers of continental Europe.

Thus we may conclude: the careful, and, as far as possible, impartial analysis of the Russian storm-cloud, has shown us that its only threatening ingredient is the autocratic power. All the rest resolves in a rain, which can bring nothing but fruit that can be welcomed by any good and upright man, whose heart beats in sympathy with his fellow-men.

And I may suggest that the benefit of the advent of freedom in Russia will not be confined to Russia alone, in the same way as the baleful influence of the Autocracy is not confined to the country directly suffering from it. Russian despotism has already done incalculable harm to the civilised world. It was the stronghold of all reaction, the supporter of oppression in all neighbouring countries. Disregarding most cynically the rights of the people, it drowned in the blood of the Hungarians the revolution of 1848 in Central Europe, one of the noblest and most promising outbursts of liberal aspirations. German unity, which would have been the dawn of better days for all the German and

Slavonic populations, had it been initiated by a free country emerging from a generous revolution—this union had to be effected by Prussian soldiers, and resulted in the creation of its "blood and iron" dictatorship, very superficially disguised by parliamentary institutions, which is another and hardly a less obstacle to the general freedom, peace, and security. At present these twin brothers—Prussian despotism, mitigated by representative forms and the high culture of the whole of the German nation; and Russian despotism, cynically brutal and not mitigated by anything—are mutually supporting and protecting each other. Their instinct of self-preservation proved stronger than the well-known racial antipathy of one of the partners and the insatiable appetite of the other, deluding the hopes of certain continental politicians; because it is too evident that they cannot exist without each other, and a severe disaster likely to involve the downfall of the one would be the ruin of both. On the day when the great German nation recovers its real and not its fictitious freedom, there will be exultation through all Russia, because the despotism destroyed in Berlin would be impossible to maintain for long in Petersburg. On the other hand, the transformation of the Northern Colossus from a gloomy centralised despotism into a vast union of self-governing states and provinces,—the only form into which a free Russia can mould itself,—will drive into a liberal evolution the whole of Central Europe. In Austria first, which otherwise will be unable to withstand for a year the great attractions of a free Russian federation on the masses of her

Slavonic population; in Germany next Prussian dictatorship will be unable to keep its hold, surrounded as it will be on all sides by free states. With it will fall the reign of brutality, encroachments, and, perhaps, the unendurable military terror now crushing and ruining all continental Europe.

Modern nations are no more isolated in their separate pursuits and interests as they were some generations back. Events taking place in one country are as quickly and as widely known in others as the events happening in a province of the latter. Provided they are of absorbing human interest, they react on the mind and the spirit of the masses as strongly as if they were happening in close vicinity. That is why we Russians, devoted to the freedom of our country, do not separate our cause from that of general liberty and democracy. We acclaim its victories in all countries, because each of them opens a better prospect for us. Our cause ought to be viewed in the same light by the thinking men of all countries. And it is certainly most reassuring to witness that among the advanced thinkers both of England and America there are many who are already viewing it in this light. " Let the Tzar and his advisers beware," says one of them, Mr. Edmund Noble, an American who has recently contributed one of the most learned and suggestive books extant on Russian things. " The spectacle of this frightfully unequal struggle—unequal alike in its justifications and in the physical forces which it arrays against each other—is not lost upon Europe, or even upon

America. . . . Already nations are beginning to recognise that the standing menace in the east of Europe is not the Russian race, but Russian absolutism. . . . Hence it is well that one can look forward to the time when a new conception of international rights and obligations shall take the place of the old; when serried lines of glistening bayonets and smoking cannon will no longer be needed to relieve the struggle for liberty from the reproach of crime; when tyranny shall be an offence against the community of nations, as it is now an offence against the community of individuals."

II.

THE RUSSIAN ARMY AND ITS COMMISSARIAT.

THE RUSSIAN ARMY AND ITS COMMISSARIAT.

I.

"A COLOSSUS with feet of clay," is the current phrase which best describes the great Power of the North. If the military strength of the Tzars were in proportion to the number of their subjects they might dispose as they pleased of the balance of European power, and Russian liberty would be a vain dream. But fortunately it is not so. With a population two and a half times greater than that of the German Empire, Russia's effective military strength is decidedly inferior to that of her Teutonic neighbours, and, relatively to her size, may be regarded as insignificant. Of this comparative weakness no better proof could be adduced than that which is afforded by the last Turkish war. Even the enemies of the Russian Government, those who were most sceptical as to the boasted extent of its resources, did not expect to see its armies held in check, beaten, and reduced to impotence by an enemy so weak and so ruined as Turkey. And when at last, after a series of defeats, Russia at length succeeded in overcoming the Ottoman armies in the field, the effort so exhausted her that she was compelled to stop in mid-career, and lost the greater part of the fruit of her sacrifices and victories—just as happened under Nicholas in the war of 1828, in similar circumstances and in the very same region. The cause of this weakness is a matter of common knowledge—at any rate in Russia. It arises, first of all, from the fact that the condition of the Imperial finances allows of the mobilisation and maintenance under arms of only a fraction of the nominal military strength of the country. In the war of 1871 Germany mustered seven-eighths of her entire military forces. In the war with Turkey the Russian Government sent into the field no more than 400,000 men, about a third of the paper strength of the active army. And these were all whom, with the utmost exertion, they could send. For the wars of these days swallow up sums so enormous that, if they be at all prolonged, the national exchequer becomes absolutely incapable of providing for the manifold wants of the forces in the field.

Yet, be that as it may, a force of 400,000 men should have amply sufficed to crush a power like Turkey, always provided that the force had been efficiently organised and well led, and if the Turks had not found in the contractors and commissariat of the Russian army their most puissant allies. Bad clothing and worse food, and the sickness thence resulting, made greater ravages in the ranks of the Russian army than the bullets of the enemy; and this state of things has prevailed without exception in every campaign in which the country has been so unfortunate as to engage.

The English reader who is familiar with Kinglake's "Invasion of the Crimea," will remember, in the chapter of the war of 1828, the author's graphic description of the diminution in the strength of the Russian regiments during the march from the interior of the country to the theatre of war. He represents it by a diagram, a fallen cone, the base of which occupies the central provinces, while the attenuated extremity rests on the Balkan Peninsula. The waste implied in this delineation was caused by the malversations of the commissariat during the long marches of the period. And the waste went on without abatement, even after the army had reached its destination and active operations were begun; for robberies are never so frequent and so easily accomplished as in a time of war. Attention is then exclusively directed to the battlefield, the central point of the contest, where the supreme struggle must be decided. "Is this the time to inquire into malversations?" said the Russian generals during the Bulgarian war, when complaints were made about the dishonesty and inefficiency of the commissariat. It is a notorious fact that army contractors may with impunity perpetrate frauds in war time which would be absolutely impossible in a time of peace—even in Russia. The depredations which every war—or, rather, the conclusion of peace—brings to light are colossal and appalling. The frauds that went on during the Crimean war, not in the army simply, —for functionaries in every branch of the national service were implicated in them—were so outrageous that they have almost passed into the domain of fable. They were continually cited as something portentous and abnormal, and an example of the enormities of bureaucratic depravity in a country cursed with serfage. When in 1877 Russia, freed from this curse, resolved to liberate the Slav population of Turkey from the Ottoman yoke, the country was in a state of great excitement. A splendid crusade was in prospect; everybody counted on an unbroken series of brilliant victories, and dwelt with pride on the progress that had been made since the Crimean war. In point of fact considerable progress had been made, and this nobody could deny. But the sequel proved that in at least one all-important particular Russia had made no advance whatever. "Amid all the patriotic excitement of the moment," wrote a St. Petersburg journal (the *Annals*, No. 234), "we begin to hear from the theatre of war voices which do not harmonise with the chorus. These voices said, at first timidly, that the army lacked this and that; some supplies being altogether wanting and others of bad quality. Then they become louder, bolder, and more frequent; and now we hear cries of sorrow and affliction—cries which are produced not by some oversight, unavoidable omission, or partial abuse, but by the actual want of daily bread. 'They gave us nothing to eat; we are dying of hunger,' is the cry from all the army. 'The preserved meats served out to us are so putrid that not alone are they unfit for food, but to prevent the outbreak of an epidemic we have to put them straightway under the ground.'"

Such were the supplies furnished by the contractors Gorvitz, Kohan, and Gregar. Similar malversations were practised in other quarters, malversations so shameless and extensive that, if they were not proved by official documents, they would be altogether incredible. The principal—almost the sole—food of Russian soldiers is black bread biscuits. Bearing this in mind, let us see what the commission of experts had to say about the biscuits supplied by the company of which Prince Uroosoff and M. Perevoshikoff were the chiefs,—a commission composed of professors of the Kieff University, from whose official report the following is an extract:—" In 100 parts of these biscuits we found an eighth part, by weight—equal to 13 per cent.—of innutritious ingredients, such as husks of grain, straw, sand, and clay." The water used in the making of them, according to the professors' report, using their very words, " was, strictly speaking, not water at all, but a red-brown liquid of high specific gravity, bearing some resemblance to cocoa with milk, and swarming with living organisms, which kept it in continual movement, thereby hindering the subsidence of inorganic matters." The factory in which these biscuits were produced (still following the report) was low and damp, and, from motives of economy, the ovens were kept at a temperature never exceeding 70° C., whereas to destroy the inferior infusoria a heat of 120° is necessary. The consequence was that all these organisms remained in the biscuits, which became breeding-places for every sort of bacteria, the creatures spreading over them and forming " a green and brown velvet-like covering." The commission absolutely refused to make any physiological experiments whatever with these precious biscuits provided by the Government of the Tzar for his valiant army. They would not give them even to dogs or swine, "being unwilling to inflict on dumb creatures the sufferings that such food must inevitably produce." Yet millions of pounds of these very biscuits were consumed by unfortunate soldiers, who, having no other food, were compelled to eat what was given to them or starve. How many deaths and how much sickness were caused by the biscuits of Prince Uroosoff, and the preserved meats of Messrs. Kohan and Gorvitz, who can say?

Other articles supplied to the army were no better than the food. In the depth of a rigorous winter the men were without overcoats, and had often to make long marches over stony ground without shoes. All Russia shuddered with pity and indignation when the story was told of the terrible winter march across the Balkans,—a march in which thousands perished of cold and exposure, and thousands more were crippled and mutilated by the frost, being forced to walk barefoot through the snow and over icy roads. The fate that befell the 24th division of General Gourko's *corps d'armée* in that cruel campaign could not be concealed; the facts were confirmed by all the war correspondents of the period, even by those of the Government press. And yet the Government assigned vast sums for clothing and feeding the army in that war, the expenditure thereon reaching a total of nearly thirty-six millions sterling. What became of all this treasure so lavishly dispensed?

But let us go on! If any have a right to careful

treatment, to good food, and comfortable quarters, they are the wounded and the sick. If any may appeal to the sentiment of our common humanity, they are again the wounded and the sick. Yet we have only to read the reports of the Sanitary Service of the Red Cross, published in two volumes by M. Abaza, red cross in the rear guard of the Russian army (1877 and 1878), and of M. Richter, red cross in the army of Bulgaria, to learn how truly horrible is the fate of wounded Russian soldiers, how cruel are the sufferings to which they are exposed. Here is an extract from the first of these reports:—

"The worst time was after the assault of Shipka. Within twelve days we received 11,000 wounded men. The small barracks literally swarmed with them. They lay in the passages between the beds, in the corridors, and on the landings. It was quite impossible to give them proper attention. But all had great need of it, and there were many bad cases. Not one had received any medical aid in the (field) hospitals. Many had only had their wounds dressed once or twice. There were no lists, and it often happened that the surgeon in charge of the convoy did not know of how many patients it was composed. When these convoys were inspected by the doctors it came frequently to pass that men were found with broken limbs destitute of splints, and nothing to hold the fractured bones together but damp and softened cardboard. . . . Owing to the absence of ambulances and the consequent impossibility of sending the wounded to other quarters there was a complete block. On the night of the 15th there came 2,704. On the following day 1,511 more came. On the night of the 16th we had 3,518, on the 17th upwards of 4,000. And for all this multitude of wounded men we had no necessaries whatever, except such as were provided by private benevolence—not a shirt, not a bandage, nothing."

Yet the Government had spent money without stint in making, as they thought, proper provision for the wounded!

And thus it was everywhere. The troops lacked everything. They had neither medicines, clothing, nor food. They were robbed right and left; the strength of the army was sapped on every side, and the difficulties of that sanguinary war, already sufficiently formidable, rendered almost insuperable. If Russian army contractors and commissariat officers did not prove too much for Russia, as in 1855, it was because of the excessive weakness of their Turkish allies. With more powerful auxiliaries they would doubtless have repeated in 1877 the victories of their predecessors in 1855. It is to them, nevertheless, that Russia owes the enormous losses of that terrible war, in which, according to the reckoning of competent authorities, there perished not fewer that 100,000 of her children. The names of the principal starvers and poisoners of the army—the chiefs of the commissariat companies—are still held in execration, and will not soon be forgotten.

II.

The exploits of the Russian commissariat are well known, even abroad. In all this there is nothing very new. That which most concerns us is to trace the relationship existing between the general system and the primary causes of the depredations which, whenever a war takes place, recur as inevitably as if they were operations of nature, and with all the regularity of the seasons. It is all very well to inveigh against Gorvitz, Varshavsky, Prince Uroosoff, and their 225 accomplices. But are they the only culpables? Why do such iniquities as theirs never occur in other armies? If contractors, in their greed of gain, deliver rations and stores of bad quality, why are they accepted as good? This is evidently the crux of the question. According to the prescriptions of the military code all articles of food and medicine delivered by a contractor have to be examined by a surgeon or a medical commission and the commandant of the corps for which they are destined, or nominees acting under his orders. Hence, without the connivance of all these people fraud would be impossible. If the contractors cheat, the brave commandant and the erudite doctors must do likewise. Not a man who went through the Bulgarian campaign would deny that this was precisely the case. On the other hand, there are always to be found in our official spheres, corrupt though they be, some men who, untainted with dishonesty, are eager to redress the wrongs which they see around them—such, for instance, as General Tcherkassoff, a military inspector. At the beginning of the campaign this officer presented to the commander-in-chief a voluminous work, in the shape of a report, in which he had collected and set forth and proved by a mass of facts, recent and palpable, the flagrant malversations and frauds of the Gorvitz company and consorts. This report, though a historical document of high value, has not yet seen the light. It was stifled by secret confederates of the implicated parties. These confederates were of all ranks, says the correspondent of the *Novoe Vremya* in his covert language. Some interrupted the reading of the report by jocular remarks which distracted attention, others protested against it as ill-timed; and, encountered everywhere with either opposition or indifference, it remained in the shade, and while the war lasted the company continued their depredations without let or hindrance. The gentlemen of the commissariat were thus not the only ones who had their fingers in the pie. War is an Eldorado for all who keep to the wall side of the road. During the trial of Rykoff, the notorious manager of the bank of Skopine, it came out that in 1877 the establishment had a considerable increase in its deposits, which came in great part from the seat of war, being lodged at high interest by officers of the commissariat and their worthy accomplices of the military branch of the service. Another characteristic fact which transpired in the course of the trial was, that when Rykoff became bankrupt, the majority of those clients declined to rank as creditors, fearing doubtless that if they did so they would be compelled to reveal the shameful secret of their ill-gotten wealth.

It is this universality of theft which provokes and maintains the malversations of army contractors. No sooner do signs of an approaching war appear on the horizon than there takes place at St. Petersburg a veritable steeplechase after contracts. To ensure the acceptance of their tenders the competitors scatter money right and left, hundreds of thousands, even millions of roubles finding their way into the pockets of people of influence, of their friends, kinsfolk, and mistresses. These gentlemen reckon, and with good warrant, on the venality of the doctors and military commanders, by whose connivance they hope to recoup the money they thus dispense, and millions in addition. On the other hand, the necessity of bribing everybody, the impossibility of making a single step without payment, obliges the contractors to take out the difference in the quality of the stores and provisions which they deliver for the use of the army. In Russia highly placed personages, as is natural, deign only to accept bribes of considerable amount. Besides a few hundred thousand roubles paid to sundry dignitaries of St. Petersburg, Rykoff had to give General Berhard a round million for looking after his business at the capital. At the beginning of the Bulgarian war all St. Petersburg was talking about a bribe of a million roubles, said to have been given by the firm of Gorvitz and Kohan to Mademoiselle Jchislov (a St. Petersburg actress, whose relations with the Grand Duke Nicholas, the elder, commander-in-chief of the army, were notorious) to secure a contract. Rumour may have exaggerated the amount in this instance; but it is quite certain that no company can obtain an extensive contract, except at an enormous outlay in bribes in the high circles. Nor is this all. Bribes have to be administered, not only in high quarters to get contracts, but all round in order to ensure acceptance of the commodities tendered by the bribers. It would, however, be a mistake to suppose that the contractors have to bribe merely when they supply articles of inferior quality. They must pay in one case as the other. You can no more get on without bribery in Russia than you can in Turkey. Bribes are a sort of homage, a compliment to which the agents of authority are so much accustomed that they regard them as a legitimate source of income. If a contractor should refuse to render the traditional tribute on the ground that his supplies were of good quality, it would be looked upon as an insult, an act of flat rebellion, and be made to cost him dear. Under one frivolous pretext or other his supplies would be rejected, and persistence in his probity would probably end in his ruin.

The commissariat service has a very evil reputation in Russia. It is no place for honest men. In his book, "A Year of War," Mr. Nemirovitch Dantchenko tells the story of a poor commissariat officer, who, unable to bear the hatred and contempt of which, in common with the service generally, he found himself the object, committed suicide. He was a man thirty-seven years old, married, and the father of a family. When the war began he held the post of tutor in one of the military gymnasiums (*corps de cadets*), but desiring to see active service he obtained the appointment of a commandant in a commissariat brigade. But, as they say in Russia, the poor man went into the water without first asking where the ford was. After two months' experience of his new position he blew out his brains at Zimnitz, in November 1877. A pathetic letter of farewell which he wrote to his wife shows clearly that the unfortunate man was driven to this desperate act by the sense of his utter powerlessness to contend with the thefts and abuses of every sort which went on around him. "The soldiers and wagoners of my brigade," he wrote, "are in rags. Their condition is deplorable. They have no tents or other shelter, and freeze as they sleep on the bare ground, and I can do nothing to help them." Another motive was the general contempt with which, as he found, the service was regarded. "The papers will tell," he wrote, "that the commandant of such and such a commissariat brigade blew out his brains, and then everybody will say, 'He robbed too recklessly, and his end is a fitting one for a scoundrel and thief.' I send thee a little money—all that remains of my pay, gained by the sweat of my brow. Not a farthing of it has been stolen from the State. But who will believe this? Oh, how everybody curses the commissariat! One is ashamed to belong to the service. I cannot bear to think of the burning hatred in which the *employés* of the department are universally held."

This sad story affords a striking illustration of the character of the Russian commissariat. As may easily be understood, no self-respecting man—save in the case of a misapprehension like that to which the unhappy officer mentioned by Nemirovitch Dantchenko fell a victim—ever dons the uniform of a commissariat *tchinovnik*, any more than that of a police officer or gendarme. Neither does he become an army contractor. There are nevertheless army contractors who feel a certain degree of repugnance for the practices which they are compelled to sanction and to follow. One of my friends, a young doctor, who shared in the first enthusiasm and deception of that unlucky war, had the opportunity of hearing the confession of one of these men. "I assure you," said to him a great contractor, a partner in the Varshavsky Company, "that it would not only be more agreeable to us, but more profitable, to furnish articles of good quality, than to scatter our money broadcast in bribes. But what can we do? The commandants and receivers insist on being paid all the same, and if the stores and other things we deliver are good they are dissatisfied; for in that case they fear they will not get so much for themselves."

I leave the reader to decide which of the two are the more to blame—the contractors, men of business, speculators by profession; or the generals, colonels commandants, and doctors of various grades, to whom the State confides its honour, who are responsible for the well-being of the army, and whose duty it is to lead against foreign foes the flower of the country.

III.

But what monsters of depravity must be these high officers and doctors, who at the hour of danger and in the face of the enemy make a shameful traffic of the health and even of the lives of their soldiers, of the men whom, by every consideration of honour and duty, they are bound to cherish and protect. No, they are not monsters. People are the creatures of habit, the slaves of custom. Things which men see being done by everybody around them they end in doing themselves, albeit these things may have seemed in the first instance utterly revolting. To understand how it is that the universal thieving which prevails in war time lies, so to speak, in the nature of things as they are in Russia, we must know what the army is in time of peace.

And about this there is no difficulty, for there is on record a whole series of trials of commandants, doctors, and military administrators, from which may be gathered some striking pictures of the life these men lead the Russian soldier, that first victim of the despotism which he sustains. Not to trench too much on the space at my disposal I limit myself to a single example, that of Dr. Skariatine, for his is a case which comprehends all the others, a faithful sample of the bulk.

Yet I would not have the reader for a moment to suppose that Dr. Skariatine, the chief figure in this trial, is one of those thieving and swindling heroes who have given their names to innumerable trials which have taken place in Russia. Dr. Skariatine found himself in the dock, not for thieving out of reason or with too much effrontery, but for his obstinacy in protesting against dishonesty which, though he could in no wise tolerate, everybody else regarded with the indifference that comes of long familiarity. The Russians are an artless and ingenuous people. Notwithstanding the experience of so many generations, there are still to be found among the functionaries of the Tzar men innocent enough to believe in the possibility of obtaining justice and redressing wrongs by bringing them under the notice of the higher authorities. In every branch of the administration there are men of this stamp, even, as an example well known in Russia proves, among the Imperial procurators themselves. These unsophisticated functionaries, it is hardly necessary to say, have no political bias; quixotism such as theirs is necessarily incompatible with subversive or anti-monarchical ideas. They have merely the sense of duty which renders it impossible for them to wink at practices which they are bound in honour to oppose and denounce. But it often enough happens that these young eagles, after one or two abortive attempts at reform, quietly fold their wings and let the world wag, neither taking part in the thefts nor exposing the thieves. "You cannot break an axe with a stick;" "It is impossible to fight where there is only one man in the field;" "He who lives with wolves must learn to howl with them;"—are they not among the most popular of Russian proverbs? Those who cannot adapt themselves to this facile philosophy always end badly; they are either expelled from the service, prosecuted, or sent to Siberia.

Dr. Skariatine, whose trial began on November 24th, 1883, was one of those unfortunate champions of duty and right. His connection with the army dated from the time of the Bulgarian war, when a crowd of young medical students, who were about finishing their final course, enrolled themselves at the call of the Government as provisional surgeons in the liberating army. From the very first, Skariatine was painfully struck by the cynical indifference to the soldiers' well-being which everywhere prevailed. As an instance of this he mentioned on his trial that once at Odessa a number of troops, in course of embarkment for the seat of war, were conveyed to the steamer *Vesta* on barges without bulwarks, the sea at the time being very rough. Skariatine and another young doctor, his comrade, pointed out to the officer in command the danger of this proceeding, suggesting at the same time that means should be taken to prevent the soldiers from being thrown into the sea by the rolling of the boat.

"What does that matter?" replied the officer. "We have enough of that sort of merchandise. A soldier is not like a horse, for the loss of which we are held responsible."

On his arrival at the seat of war, the young doctor was soon made aware of the malversations which were practised at the expense of the troops. His protests were frequent and energetic, but nothing of course came of them. In the hospitals, for instance, the soldiers were robbed, not only of food and medicines, but of their very pocket-money. There is a regulation which prescribes that, in order to hinder the sick from buying things which might injure their health, they must, on their entrance into the hospital, give up to the administration all the money in their possession. This regulation is rigorously enforced. But when they leave the hospital, the soldiers, "in the majority of cases," says Skariatine, are unable to get their money back, beg and insist as they may. He told before the tribunal that, being one day in hospital No. 11, he took the part of a young soldier who was begging with hot tears that the seven roubles (fourteen shillings), of which he had been deprived when he entered, might be returned to him. All that the doctor got for his pains was a recommendation to mind his own business. When the Inspector-General Priselkoff made his official visit, Skariatine complained to him of these and other abuses, and the former was so moved by his statement that he drew forth his notebook in order to put down the names of the delinquents. But so soon as he heard the name of the principal depredator, the general closed his book with the exclamation, " Malenine! Oh, I can do nothing against him. He is a man of influence. He won't let himself be caught."

The Government and soldiers were robbed with equal cynicism and the most complete impartiality. While giving his evidence, Skariatine related that he had actually seen wood burnt instead of infected clothing, linen, and so forth, which, having been used for contagious cases in the hospital, was ordered to be destroyed. The articles supposed to have been burnt were then entered in the accounts as newly acquired, and, of course, reissued, and paid for a second time.

The war over, the young doctor returned to St. Petersburg to finish his studies. "I thought," he said, in presence of his judges, "that it was only in Turkey that the dregs of society could rise to the surface, and I was under the impression that the things which took place in that country were impossible in Russia. This is the reason why, having finished my course in the School of Medicine, I again, despite my unfortunate experience in the war, joined the army, hoping that I might thereby be able to do something towards improving the lot of our soldiers. But I cruelly deceived myself."

In effect, Skariatine was appointed assistant surgeon in the Ninth Regiment of Uhlans, then quartered at Lubno, and at once addressed himself to his modest task with all the energy and zeal of youth. A multitude of witnesses testified that the young doctor occupied himself exclusively with his patients. He made no acquaintances; he was never seen outside the sphere of his duties. All his days, from sunrise to nightfall, were passed in the hospital. He bought with his own means medicines for the sick soldiers, and gave himself heart and soul to his work. A man so devoted to duty could not fail from the first to fall foul of the abuses and malversations of which the regimental hospital was a very hotbed. Like all other Russian hospitals, military and general, that of which Skariatine had charge was divided into two departments, the lazaretto, or hospital proper, for serious cases, and the okolotok, or consulting division, for the treatment of unimportant cases. But the expenditure reports apply only to the former department, that of the lazaretto; the inspectors presuming that the okolotoks, not being counted as really sick, do not require medicine. By an ingenious device the superior officers, in collusion with the doctors, turn this arrangement to account Colonels of regiments and generals of divisions find it greatly to their advantage to have the lowest possible number of sick figuring in their reports. A low sick list brings them credit; it is regarded as an unfailing test of the comfort and health of the men and the care exercised by the military and medical officers in the matters of food and sanitation. To obtain this result, and ensure the commendation of the Minister of War, or, to use the current phrase, "in order not to spoil the reports," the okolotok is crowded with serious cases which are written down as trivial, although it is provided neither with suitable beds, linen, nor food. In August 1881, when typhoid fever in an almost epidemic form broke out in the Ninth Uhlan Regiment, thirty patients were placed in the okolotok, and, albeit some of them were suffering from dysentery, they had no medicines nor any other nourishment than the coarse food which is given to Russian soldiers in a normal state of health. Yet at the very same time there were twenty-four vacant beds in the lazaretto, kept so, "not to spoil the reports" with too many sick. When Skariatine, in the absence of the senior surgeon, had the more serious cases removed to the lazaretto, he was severely reprimanded, and to prevent a repetition of the proceeding the chief surgeon took the okolotok out of his hands altogether, leaving in his charge only the half-empty hospital.

The desire to have the smallest possible number of sick—on paper—by no means implies that any special pains are taken to cure those who are ill. During Skariatine's two years' service the regimental pharmacy was quite destitute of medicines. The senior surgeon, fearing to give offence to the heads of the department, to whom the supply of medical stores and hospital requisites is a lucrative source of income, refused to ask for any. In these circumstances it became necessary to obtain a supply of drugs from the local pharmacy. But for this purpose, and inclusive of special food and so forth for the patients, Colonel Goriatcheff, the commander of the regiment, would allow no more than £10 a year; at the very time, too, when he had in his possession £7,000 saved from the regimental allowances and appropriated to his own use. This sordid economy in requisites for the sick obtains more or less throughout the service, and the system of doing everything for show, cloaking up evils—often very real and serious evils—for fear of "spoiling reports" and causing displeasure in high quarters, is simply universal in Russia, the country where bureaucracy reigns supreme. Such incidents as those I have described are of daily occurrence in every *corps d'armée*. An acquaintance of my own, an army surgeon, was transferred from Kieff to Vinnizy, an insignificant provincial town, for having, in spite of several reprimands, dispensed too much medicine in the hospital under his charge, and, above all, because he insisted on taking prompt and energetic measures to stamp out a malady of the eyes, which had all the characteristics of an epidemic. The colonel wished to conceal the fact from his superiors, even at the risk of letting it become more virulent and extensive. But not content with giving out the necessary quantity of linen and the rest, the surgeon took it upon him to write to the heads of the Medical Department, apprising them of the outbreak, and calling attention to the danger which it involved. Then they sent him away. His importunity had become intolerable. But I should be in no way surprised to hear of him being one day in the dock, like Skariatine.

This double system has given rise to a general and curious anomaly, yet the facts are easy of verification—the great mortality in the Russian army, as compared with the seemingly small number of sick. The authorities would doubtless like to obtain satisfactory tables of mortality by concealing deaths. But that is beyond their power. According to the Russian Calendar for 1880, the death-rate in the Tzar's army is 14·73 per 1,000—an enormous proportion for men in the prime of life. In the English army the proportion is 8, in the Prussian army only 6 per 1,000. But if we were to judge by its sick lists alone, we should conclude that the Russian army was the healthiest in Europe, for of 1,000 men there are no more than 600 (the okolotoks included) who in the course of a year have occasion to consult the doctor. In the French army, on the other hand, the proportion is 1,965; that is to say, every soldier sees the doctor on the average twice in a twelvemonth. In the Prussian army the average is 1,496. We have consequently this startling contradiction—nearly twice as many deaths as in other armies, and twice-thrice fewer cases of sickness. It results from this consideration alone that Russian soldiers either receive no medical care worth mentioning or that the official reports are garbled. As a matter of fact, and as we have seen, both these conditions obtain in the army of the Tzar. The rogueries and other malpractices that went on in the hospital were not the only abuses which

Skariatine's trial brought to light, nor was it with regard to them that the contest which ended in his trial arose. The young doctor got out of the principal difficulty by buying medicines with his own money. But other abuses were past curing by any such expedient. The soldiers were plundered right and left. Everybody stole "according to his rank," to adopt an expressive Russian phrase. The colonel took his stealings from the regimental chest. The squadron commanders took what they could get out of the sums assigned for their squadrons, and the non-commissioned officers picked up the crumbs which fell from the tables of their superiors in rank. When the official inquiry took place, it was proved that the commander of the first squadron economised on his men's rations to such an extent that he literally starved them. He appropriated even the wretched pittance of two shillings a quarter, which the Russian Government allows its soldiers, and calls their pay, and took without scruple the money remitted them by their kinsfolk through the post. Yet the men, slaves of discipline, hardly ever protested against the malversations which cost them so dear, for the officers of a regiment have a thousand ways of evading responsibility, and of taking cruel vengeance on those who dare to murmur or complain. The higher authorities, moreover, are little disposed to " endanger discipline " by listening to the accusations of subordinates against their chiefs; but a worm will turn, and a time came when the patience of the soldiers of the 9th Regiment was exhausted. At a review held by the commander of the division, General Korevo, the soldiers of Matveenko's squadron made formal complaint against him. It was in vain that the under officers, faithful to their chief, ran behind the ranks whispering fierce threats, and reminding the men that the general was there to-day but that they would be masters on the morrow. The victims refused to be silenced. (When, after a review, soldiers are asked if they have any complaints to make, the commissioned officers leave the ranks, while the non-commissioned officers, being regarded as simple soldiers, remain.) The complaint was made, and a young subaltern of the name of Sytchevsky, questioned by the general, confirmed the statement of the men. All the same nothing was done. Sytchevsky was even, under some frivolous pretext, submitted to disciplinary punishment. As for the two principal delinquents, Matveenko and Kopatch, against whose malversations the soldiers had protested, they were both shortly afterwards promoted, the former to the command of a regiment. These indisputable proofs of the connivance of the higher authorities in the abuses he had denounced did not, however, suffice to quench the reforming zeal of the unfortunate doctor. And it would not be easy, in the presence of such enormities as prevailed in the 9th Regiment of Uhlans, to silence any man not lost to all sense of duty and dignity. The officers, not content with starving their men, crippled them. Evidence was given on the trial of eight cases of lameness, resulting from blows inflicted on the men by their officers, from the sergeants and corporals to Colonel Goriatcheff himself. The occasion was always some absurdly trivial offence, such as a military salute clumsily given, a military exercise insufficiently learnt. Skariatine, who saw men brought into the hospital bleeding from the mouth and ears, sometimes insensible and with broken limbs, perhaps crippled for life—Skariatine, unable to contain his indignation, protested warmly against these infamies, and was backed by the younger officers of the regiment, but the movement, opposed by the superior officers and their clique, came to nothing. True, Colonel Goriatcheff resigned, but to command a division, not to answer for his misdeeds before a court martial. His successor was the late Colonel Brevern, and to him also Skariatine complained of the barbarous way in which the soldiers were treated. But the new colonel had the impudence to answer in these words, as was testified by several witnesses: "Russian soldiers must be beaten and knocked about, otherwise you can do nothing with them." To prevent as far as possible any further interference on the part of the young doctor, Colonel Brevern ordered that no soldier who was beaten into a state of insensibility should be taken to the hospital. On this Skariatine made a formal complaint to General Tejelnikoff, commander of the division. The answer was given before the regiment, after a review. "Disciplinary punishments are for imbeciles," said the general; "with a good soldier you must use your fists."

This peremptory argument did not convince Skariatine. After failing with the general, he made a complaint in due form to the surgeon-in-chief of the division, supporting his charge with numerous well-authenticated facts. On this a series of intrigues, directed by Colonel Brevern, with the object of ruining Skariatine, were begun. It were useless to recount them. But in any case it was necessary to take legal cognisance of his charges. A judge was sent to Lubny to verify the statements he had made. Several officers, Gichareff, Savenkoff, Damlovsky, and Sytcheff, fully confirmed the doctor's depositions. It may be supposed that a plaint so powerfully supported could not remain without effect. Nor did it; but in the contrary sense. The general commanding the division made a pretext for presenting himself at Lubny, called together the officers, told them that "a scoundrel" (this in allusion to Skariatine) "had come among them," and set himself to bellow against everybody, conduct in which several officers had not been ashamed to countenance him. "In my opinion," he went on, "these officers should be expelled from the regiment as scabby lambs are turned out of a flock of sheep." And this was actually done. A short time afterwards the four officers in question were expelled from the 9th Regiment of Uhlans. But even yet Skariatine would not be quiet. He refused to howl with the wolves, and, though alone and unsupported, continued the struggle. He appealed to the Minister of War three times without effect, and only after surmounting a crowd of obstacles did he succeed in getting his memoir into his Excellency's hands. Then he had to make five separate applications before he could obtain his answer. In the end, however, he did obtain it. The minister offered, if Skariatine would withdraw his memoir, to liberate him from the service from which, being stipendiary of the Government, he could not retire without permission. "It is not for that I presented my memoir," answered the doctor, and he categorically refused to sell his connivance even for a bribe so delicately offered. On this the minister issued an order " to expel Skariatine from the regiment, and send him to serve in some hospital."

It was only then that the optimism of the young doctor, who up to this point had maintained unswerving faith in the integrity of his country's Government, broke down. He was so much affected by his repeated failures and the discovery that there is no justice under the rule of the Tzar that he fell seriously ill. When he recovered he received an order to betake himself to the Bobrouisk hospital. Skariatine declined to obey this order, and addressed to the minister a report justifying his resolution, on the ground that "he refused to serve in any place whatever, being convinced that the position of a surgeon under the Ministry of War is incompatible with the conscientious fulfilment of his duties and the engagements into which he enters when taking the oath of service.' It was this declaration—a declaration regarded by his superiors as utterly outrageous and monstrous—which caused Skariatine to be put on his trial, and led to the revelations I have described.

* * * * *

Skariatine's trial is like a window left open for a moment, through which may be seen the general and normal condition of the Russian army. That which this trial reveals is done more or less every where. The difference is simply that there is not everywhere a man of Skariatine's calibre to denounce the wrong and lift the veil by which it is hidden. The senior surgeon, Konstantinoff, did not, when Skariatine made his first complaint, say to him paternally, "Why do you give yourself so much trouble, my dear fellow? We all see the things that you see, but we hold our tongues. Why do you want to be cleverer than others?" And the Imperial Procurator, who conducted the prosecution, could not refrain from ridiculing "this Don Quixote, who fancies that the abuses which prevail in the army are unknown to the Government." He was quite right. The Government, or, at any rate, the members of the headquarter staff, who have served in every rank, cannot ignore the things that are known to every greenhorn of an officer who has been a year in the army. In Russia the command of a regiment is a sinecure—as sure a source of income as a landed estate. These "incomes" are made in a variety of ways; from "economies" effected in the purchase of food, forage, saddlery, and the rest, down to the very soles of the soldiers' boots. Food, being in daily consumption, and its consumption less easily checked than some other things, is the principal source of revenue.

There is another matter which it is equally instructive to observe. Skariatine's trial shows how that principle of natural selection, which under the present *régime* prevails throughout the administration, operates in the army. The general body of officers, as we have already mentioned, do not in Russia represent any particular class or caste. Russia is a country essentially democratic. It has nothing even remotely resembling the military aristocracy of Prussia, or, in a less degree, of Austria. With the exception of a few privileged corps of the Guard, officered by the aristocracy of the Court, the Russian army obtains its officers from that inferior nobility and that "little *bourgeoisie*" who are the chief repositories and representatives of progressive ideas. A considerable proportion of these officers receive their education in the Military Gymnasium and the five colleges of St. Petersburg and Moscow, good secondary schools, which give a general, as well as a special, education. Russia might easily secure for its army a body of officers as honest and as zealous for the good of their country as any other state. Of this the present wide diffusion of revolutionary ideas among the officers of every arm is the very best proof. If there are found so many officers ready to risk their future and endanger their lives in the hope of freeing their country from the yoke of a barbarous Government, there would, of a surety, be found ten times as many willing to render her the modest meed of honest service. But that which the existing *régime* does wherever its influence extends, it does also in the army; it represses the better elements to encourage dishonesty, egoism, peculation, and rapine. Officers like Sytchevsky, Gichareff, and others, who understand honour in the sense in which it is understood elsewhere, are either expelled from the army, or, weary of sterile struggles and outraged past bearing by the spectacle of daily infamies, leave the service *en masse*. Others, more energetic, espouse the cause of revolution, and retain their positions in order that, on the first occasion, they may employ their arms for the delivery of their country. The Goriatcheffs, the Kopatches, the Matveenkos, they alone, possessing as they do all the qualities which enable men in the Russian army to rise, have the best chance of advancement; and, once they reach the higher grades, they have only to bring into play that terrible instrument known as military discipline to hush up their common peculations and set detection at defiance. And these gentlemen, accustomed as they are to rob their soldiers and the State in a time of peace, how can they abandon their malpractices at a time when, by reason of increased expenditure and relaxed control, thieving is abnormally easy and profitable?

IV.

So much for the strictly military officers and the Commissariat. In order to complete our picture it is only necessary to say a few words concerning the medical department, which, in peace as well as in war, plays so important a part in the malversations of which the army is the theatre. To give an idea of the character of our medical service two recent and characteristic trials may be cited—that of Bush and that of Koritzky. Both these men were fully matriculated thieves. The first was Surgeon-in-Chief of the Fleet. His trial took place in 1882, and made, as well it might, a great noise in Russia. The other gentleman was Surgeon-in-Chief of the

Army. His trial took place in December 1884. The two trials in their main features were identical—the same crimes, the same procedure, the same subterfuges of defence. We need then analyse but one of these trials,—that of Bush,—for, though older than the other, it is richer in detail. Surgeon-in-Chief and Civil-General, Dr. Bush did not, like Rykoff, of the Skopine Bank, distinguish himself by the enormity of his peculations; the blackmail he levied never exceeded from a hundred to two hundred pounds, and he condescended, on occasion, to accept as little as a five-pound note. Neither did he show in his rogueries any peculiar cleverness and *finesse*. The most characteristic feature in the Bush affair is its amazing and patriarchal simplicity. For eight years places, promotions, and transfers were sold in the chief surgeon's office without any sort of concealment or disguise, almost as openly as if they had been offered by auction. True, the director did not actually receive the cash with his own hands. But that made practically no difference. It even simplified matters. The business was managed by two confidential men—Andreef, who acted as cash-keeper, and Parfenoff, who acted as clerk. It was no secret; everybody knew what was going on. Of one hundred and twenty-six surgeons who were called as witnesses, eighty-six admitted that they had either paid blackmail themselves or knew those who had been thus mulcted. The other forty denied all personal knowledge of the doings in question: protested even that they had never heard tell of them. But their sincerity was doubted by the Imperial Procurator, who complimented the eighty-six on the "civic courage" (*sic*) which they displayed in confessing their fault. And there is good reason to believe that the Procurator's scepticism was not without warrant. Dr. Saviesheff and Dr. Lukine testified that "everybody said that Andreef, Bush's man of business, took bribes." The fact was known even to the students of the Academy of Medicine. Doctor-Inspector Popoff testified to having heard students of the previous year speak of it as matter of common knowledge, and he had said sharply to one of them, "Don't talk nonsense. How can you pay for an appointment when you have not a kopeck in your pocket?" On this, the student, nothing disconcerted, made this answer, "Oh, that is nothing. If I cannot give money I can give a bill." So the young disciples of Æsculapius were already familiar with the mysteries of "making paper" and the procedure of semi-official bribery. The bill system was only one practicable for impecunious doctors, emulous of good places and fat pay. One of the witnesses mentioned, among other things, that, according to public rumour, Andreef always conducted his questionable business "like a gentleman." The bills, which he took beforehand, were never presented for payment until the promises in consideration of which they were accepted had been fulfilled. If, on the other hand, Bush was not able to keep his engagement, the bill was returned—a curious instance of the "honour" which is said to prevail among thieves. Both parties to these nefarious transactions acknowledged a certain conventional standard of honesty to which they felt themselves bound to conform.

As a further illustration, take the case of Dr. Malinovsky. He undertook to pay Andreef, acting on behalf of Bush, 400 roubles for a place at Vladivostock. Bush asked for no other security than the aspirant's word, received him "very graciously," promised him the nomination he wanted, and in dismissing him gave him a cordial shake of the hand. But when Malinovsky's appointment was gazetted as medical officer at Vladivostock, and he received travelling money for his journey (out of which Bush's fee was to have been deducted), he did not pay up. This did not arise from any want of will, but, as the young doctor testified in court, it was absolutely impossible for him to spare just then the sum he had agreed to give. Before leaving St. Petersburg he went to Bush, explained his circumstances, apologised for his unpunctuality, and promised to pay later on. But Bush would not listen to reason, made "a great row," and showed Malinovsky to the door, crying furiously, "If I had known you were such a scoundrel, you should never have entered the service." After this, as may be supposed, the Surgeon-in-Chief did not get his 400 roubles. But Malinovsky felt that he had not acted quite uprightly in the matter; his conscience always troubled him, and he declared before the tribunal that he still considered himself Bush's debtor. But most of the doctors paid up in due course, either out of a sense of honour, or to avoid incurring the enmity of their chief. Ordinary nominations and simple transfers were dealt in "according to the established tariff," which varied, however, from 200 to 400 roubles (£20 to £40) for each transaction.

Bush, of course, endeavoured to exact the larger sum, and drove very hard bargains. The Surgeon-General of the Baltic Fleet, V. Smirnoff, testified that in 1880 he was travelling with two young doctors, one of whom, unrestrained by his presence, observed, "But it is altogether abominable. They bargain down there (the Surgeon-in-Chief's office) as if it were a drug shop. I offered Andreef 250 roubles, but he wanted 300, and as I could not afford so much my nomination did not come off." Yet all was not "shop." The story was graced with a touch of poetry and romance, represented by Mdlle. Selezneff, a lady of the *corps de ballet*. Mr. Efrenoff, one of the witnesses, testified that, being invited to take tea at Bush's house, he met there the lady in question and Andreef. While they were at table a packet was brought to the chief, who, after opening it and running his eye over the contents, exclaimed, "Ah, what a stupid fellow this Shvank is! He does not know how to make appointments." And then, turning to Mdlle. Selezneff, he said, "Nominate somebody yourself," whereupon the ballet dancer named Dr. Tichoff, and her nomination was duly carried into effect.

Most of the posts at Bush's disposal were sold for lump sums, but there were others from which he drew a regular yearly income. In Russia, as everybody is well aware, a naval or military hospital is a small gold mine for those who know how to make the most of their opportunities. So many things are required, and it is easy, either by minimising the quantities or deteriorating the quality,—perhaps by both,—to "save" something on every one of them. For "save" read "steal." This being the case, it is not surprising that the directorship of a naval or military hospital should fetch a relatively high price—two, three, and even four thousand roubles. But Bush, not satisfied with a payment down, levied on his nominees an annual tribute, and if they fell behind with their payments, or did not pay what he thought enough, the Surgeon-in-Chief would threaten them with dismissal. As, moreover, he knew every detail of hospital administration, and could gauge to a nicety how much every directorship was worth, it was impossible to keep back any part of the plunder which he considered rightly his due. There was found among his papers a detailed list of the income of Cronstadt hospital, expressly drawn up for his information by his confidential clerk, Parfenoff. Its extent may be inferred from the fact that it covered two folios of foolscap. Nothing was omitted. Bush was equally familiar with what may be termed the interior or domestic bribery of the hospitals. In his own particular note-book was found the following interesting memorandum:—"Grinzevitch (the director of a hospital) receives bribes from the doctors through the intermediary of the clerk Terentieff; from the furnishers of food and firewood through the intermediary of the clerk Makaroff; from the furnishers of the pharmacy through Skopenhalen; from those of the school of surgery through Akinfieff."

Thus Grinzevitch did in his hospital precisely what Bush himself did in his more exalted sphere. Each for himself, according to the measure of his ability. And this went on for long years. And even the trial, when it did come to pass, was the result of pure accident. A functionary so highly placed that he could not be hushed up—General Dr. Vakulovsky—fell out with Bush and denounced him in due form and had him prosecuted.

Dr. Krivouchev, one of the witnesses, threw a side light on the customs of other departments which revealed some curious facts. This young doctor told that, after taking his degree, he made the tour of all the departments, "and that everywhere it was the same thing." In one he was informed bluntly that he must pay blackmail. In others the fashion was to say nothing, but to write on a piece of paper or trace with the finger on the window glass the amount he was required to pay—always a considerable sum, "more, even, than Bush was in the habit of exacting from his clients." And Dr. Krivouchev's comrade, Dr. Karst, avowed frankly that "in the Ministry of War (territorial) still higher bribes were demanded." On the trial of Dr. Koritzky (a second Bush) the testimony of the latter witness in this regard was fully confirmed. When three young surgeons, who had bribed their way to lucrative posts, arrived at Cronstadt, the young sailor officers asked them openly "how much their places had cost them," adding, "You are luckier than we. You get what you pay for, but with us (the Ministry of Marine) they make us pay and give us nothing for our money."

This trial of Bush, equally with that of Rykoff, is a mirror in which we see reflected all the rottenness of Russian official life. As a journal of the day observed, "It is a lump of mud taken at random from a marsh reeking with filth." There are Bushes everywhere, big and little. And every Bush has his Parfenoff, his Andreef, and his Mdlle. Selezneff. But I shall not dwell here on the social and political significance of this scandalous trial. Let us confine ourselves rather to what may be termed its special and technical bearings, so far as they throw a light on the subject more immediately before us. The case of Dr. Bush enables us to see in action that process of natural selection of which I cited several instances in connection with the army. It may, indeed, be safely affirmed that this process has gone further in the department of medicine than that of arms. We have seen by what sort of disgraceful openings men enter on the noble career of healing, and by what means they rise therein. Appointments, promotions, exchanges—all are obtained by bribery. Yet a man who pays for a favour or a place is not necessarily a scoundrel,—at any rate, in Russia,—for in Russia bribery has become, so to speak, acclimatised; it holds a recognised place among our manners and customs. But, even with this qualification, a briber cannot be regarded as a model of civic virtue, and those who, though they may not actually either bribe or take bribes, never raise their voices in protest against the malversations and abuses of others, do not occupy a much loftier position. If not robbers they are concealers, and the line that divides the man who, by keeping silence, makes himself a virtual accomplice, from the active associate is easily trespassed. And if by chance an honest doctor gets in by honourable means, and is zealous for the public weal, as Skariatine was, it is much more difficult for him to remain in an inferior position and keep his integrity than for a military officer of the combatant branch of the service. For a doctor is naturally a controller and a chief. It is his duty to watch over and safeguard the well-being of the soldier. Hence his part must either be connivance and complicity, or war to the knife against an entire system, a war *à la* Skariatine, which can only end as his ended.

I would not suggest that all our naval and military doctors are dishonest, any more than I would say that all our superior officers are like Goriatcheff and Matveeff. Yet it is beyond dispute that Bush and Koritzky, Grinzevitch and Konstantinoff, are the natural and logical outcome of the conditions we have described; and it is equally beyond dispute that in times of war we can expect but a repetition on a greater scale of the things that are done during peace.

The colossal and universal robberies of which the Russian army was the victim in the Bulgarian war, as previously in the Crimean war, were not, let me repeat, due merely to the bad faith of roguish contractors, any more than to the fortuitous negligence or incompetence of generals and inspectors. The cause lies deeper. They were the natural results of our political system. For this reason that which has befallen in the past will happen in the future. Before the Bulgarian war, as I have already observed, the Russian people were under a fond illusion in this regard. But they are under no such illusion now. Bitter experience has opened their eyes to the truth. From the first rumour of a possible war with

England Russian papers have told us frankly what to expect. And all Russia is of the same opinion. In the next war, against whomsoever it may be waged, the soldiers will either be starved or poisoned, either be compelled to eat adulterated bread and putrid meat, or die of hunger; wounded, they will be left without help, without covering, and without shelter. They will perish by thousands of exposure and disease; they will be forced to march barefoot (because the contractors will deliver shoes to the men after, not before, a battle, it being judiciously calculated that, as many soldiers are sure to be killed, a considerable saving will thereby be effected—not to the State however). They will either get no medicines at all, or drugs that are not medicines,— cream of tartar instead of quinine,—the difference in price going into the pockets of those who are appointed to watch over their health and cure their ills.

But is it needful to say that an army, however numerous and courageous it may be, eaten up by evils such as these, is utterly incapable of waging a long and serious war? Herein lies the cause of the relative weakness of Russia. By raising an enormous loan, and so imperilling the nation's future and burdening beyond measure its resources, the financial difficulty may be temporarily surmounted. But against the gangrene which is gnawing away at its heart the present *régime* is utterly impotent to contend. How can it protect the private soldier from his own chiefs and doctors? It is an entire *personnel* that needs purifying: it is the system, which has made them what they are, that must be remodelled and renewed. As things are, the evil can only increase. The antagonism between the autocracy and the instructed forces of the nation grows more virulent year by year, the army itself included.

The existing Government has thus corrupted, little by little, the entire body social. The autocracy is as incompatible with the safety of the State as with the peace of other nations. Though a military *régime par excellence*, instituted with the intention and object of waging wars of conquest, and likely to grow more warlike in proportion to its interior decomposition, the autocracy is actually the cause of the present military weakening of the State, as much as it is the cause of its extreme poverty and of the stoppage of all intellectual progress. The military courage and carelessness for life of Russian people, having in it something of oriental fatalism, combined with a power of enduring privations which no European soldiers would ever bear, have enabled the Russian army to accomplish many high feats of arms, and to acquire a well-earned military reputation. It is, and will always be, a tremendous foe in open encounters. But it is quite unfit for a long and serious war. I remember an English colonel, who as a member of the Afghan Boundary Commission had good opportunity of observing our soldiers in Central Asia, saying to me, " The Russian soldiers could have conquered the world but for a good commissariat." When they will have such an one Russia will not want any more to conquer anybody. And in its present condition it is doubtful whether our army would be able to defend the frontier in the case of a great continental war.

III.

THE YOUNG POLAND AND RUSSIAN REVOLUTION.

THE YOUNG POLAND AND RUSSIAN REVOLUTION.

I.

IT was in the beginning of 1879 that I had the first opportunity of seeing the Polish revolutionists in their own homes. Early in the morning the St. Petersburg train stopped at the beautiful northern railway station of Warsaw. I was not alone, having for fellow-traveller a Polish revolutionist, whom I always called Michael. Whether this was his Christian name or not I do not know. During our short acquaintance he has changed his name no less than half a dozen times, and most probably had forgotten himself what his real one was. It was quite pardonable, therefore, that I was not more clear on this subject than himself. What I did know of him was, that he was one of the initiators of the new Polish revolutionary movement, and one of the active members of the young revolutionary association. Now we travelled together, and stopped at Warsaw because he promised to introduce me to all his friends in that town—a most welcome promise, that any Russian revolutionist would have willingly accepted, as I did.

In 1879 the police severity was already in all its vigour, and it would have been surprising had things been better in Warsaw than elsewhere. We had hardly time to enter our room at the hotel, when we were asked for our passports, and subjected to the minutest examination as to the object of our journey, the time we proposed to stay in the town, and many other particulars. This would have seemed very indiscreet to peaceful citizens, but not to us, of course. By giving a little play to our imagination, we satisfied with the greatest ease the curiosity of the police. As there was in the register book a blank line, over which stood the word "character," which means in Polish "occupation," but in Russian "temper," it allowed me the opportunity of pushing my frankness to the extent of declaring in answer that we were both kind-tempered and most pacific men. The waiter, not being thoroughly versed in Russian, could not see the joke, and so the register passed to the office. Our passports were taken from us, also to be handed over that very hour to the police for examination and verification. The passports were home-made, of course. But having already undergone many verifications, both had their backs covered with as many police stamps, acknowledging most peremptorily the incomparable skill of my friend Alexis O—— and Mdlle. Alexandrine M——, who presided then over the Nihilistic passport department. We had not the slightest doubt that our papers would pass the ordeal quite safely, and return early on the morrow with additional marks of their good quality.

Michael had a great deal of business, all equally "urgent," to perform. I knew that on attending to each detail he would find a number of details growing out of it, and would try to do them at once. Nevertheless, he promised to be back in two hours, and to arrange in the meantime all the appointments —a thing very complicated in Russia. To my great surprise he arrived only one hour and a half behind the time he had fixed. We started at once, and went into the streets—the celebrated streets of the Polish capital, which have seen so much greatness and so many sorrows. Michael was my guide, and, as we proceeded, explained to me the memories connected with the places we were passing. A long and pathetic record it was. Here was erected the first barricade in 1830, where a handful of Polish boys made head against the battalions of the Tzar. There, in 1863, the Cossacks attacked a crowd of unarmed people going to church; women were pierced through with pikes, and babies trampled down under horses' hoofs. A little farther, in a small thoroughfare, a Russian policeman was killed in open daylight by some bold avenger; and here a Polish patriot put to death before the eyes of his wife and children. We could hardly take a hundred steps without my companion raising before my imagination some deed of valour or self-sacrifice of martyrdom. A sense of dread overpowered me. There is no city in the world whose soil is so bloody as Warsaw. It seemed as if every stone of the pavement we trod, under the dirt and snow covering it, must have had its stain of martyrs' blood. I understood then why Warsaw has been and will always be the site of revolution. Until it is burnt to ashes and destroyed, the plough passed over its ruins, and its citizens not allowed to settle within a score of miles, as with old Carthage—until then Warsaw may be reduced to gloomy silence, but never subdued by despotism; and at the first call of liberty they will rise in arms as one man.

I will not speak of all with whom I became acquainted on that day and in the three following, which I could not refrain from passing in this town. I will dwell only on one particular which struck me most: the character of the socialist movement among the workmen was, indeed, the chief object of the new revolutionary party. The day after our arrival at Warsaw, Michael and another Polish revolutionist—the engineer W——, with whom I was connected in St. Petersburg—came to my hotel, and said they would accompany me to a workmen's meeting to be held—secretly, of course—in one of the democratic quarters of the town.

After some rambling through the narrow streets, we entered a vast court-yard, at one corner of which stood a large one-storied house. Heaps of rough boards were laid on the ground, or stood erect against the walls. It was a joiner's shop. The meeting was to be held in a back chamber. When we entered the ante-room, we could hear the hum of voices. There were, however, but few persons assembled. We came early, and could indulge in conversation, which gave me the opportunity of knowing these people better. After being presented by Michael and W—— as a Russian revolutionist, I was welcomed as a friend and brother. There was not the slightest shadow of national distrust of a Russian in their hearty frankness. Many misfortunes were due in former times to such distrust.

Two generations ago it separated by the space of five years two great revolutions,—that of 1825 of St. Petersburg, and that of 1830 in Warsaw,—which, united, would have been decisive. Even a generation later, in the insurrection of 1863, as our fathers in revolution, Herzen and Bakounin, complain, it was the insuperable obstacle to a good understanding between Russian and Polish democrats.

I knew perfectly well that this distrust had entirely disappeared among educated revolutionists. But I was most pleasantly surprised to see that it was just the same with simple workmen.

When all had assembled, there were altogether some fifteen to eighteen people. It was a meeting of delegates or organisers, each of whom represented a circle of fifteen to twenty persons. Thus at that moment there must have been about 150 to 200 workmen united in one organisation—a number that surprised me, indeed; for I knew that all this had been done in a few months, and that eighteen months before there was not a single socialist circle among the Warsaw workmen. I remembered that when we Russian revolutionists began our propaganda in St. Petersburg in 1871, at the end of the first two years we could hardly contrive to impart to a dozen workmen the notions of socialism. Only in 1879, after nine years' exertion, the first strong and serious workmen's organisation, called the Northern League, was founded. The difference in the results seemed still more surprising when one compared the respective forces that began the movement in the two countries. At St. Petersburg the number of propagandists belonging to the instructed classes—let us say of students, although the term is not quite exact—was so great, that in the first four or five years of propaganda we may reckon without exaggeration at least three propagandist students who have spent their forces to gain over one socialist of the working classes. In Warsaw it was quite the reverse. The 150 to 200 socialists, united in a few months into one association, were the result of the work of only three agitators of the educated classes. All these three propagandists I knew. They were very devoted, energetic persons; but they were not at all superior to those of St. Petersburg, among whom there were many people of longer experience.

Their wonderfully quick success was, therefore, only an illustration and a measure of the great difference in the material on which they had to work.

Its rapidity of expansion was not, however, the chief feature of the Warsaw socialist movement. W—— and Michael told me that all the propaganda was carried out now entirely by the workmen themselves. The three initiators had some difficulty in organising the first circle of workmen; but when once they had formed a small group of five to seven workmen, the latter in no time acquired numerous adherents among their companions, organised new circles, and carried the propaganda further without any assistance from their educated companions. When any circle grew too large it divided itself into two, and, in order to keep in communication with the whole association, elected a delegate to a separate circle of a superior order, having its regular meetings, and entrusted with the general direction and supervision. The delegates or "organisers" in various quarters of the town held small local meetings to provide for the wants of their district, and had their general as well as particular funds, small libraries composed of clandestine publications, and so forth. The organisation worked like a well-constructed machine.

All this is very simple, of course. If asked to draw up a scheme of a working men's organisation, every propagandist would have proposed just the same. But it is one thing to write out a scheme and quite another to put it into practice. For us Russian revolutionists the greatest difficulty was the organising of our workmen. If we succeeded in moving some three or four score of adherents, it was a herculean task to put them, so to say, into rank; to introduce order into their gregarious mass; to place them in conspiratory array,—which, by dividing functions, divides peril,—and in restricting the intercourse the sphere of activity of each single part strengthens the power of resistance and effectiveness of the whole conspiracy. The Polish propagandist has no such difficulty. Their workmen seem to have been already educated for conspiracies, as soldiers are drilled for war. They had only to be called out and put in motion; the placing them in ranks went by itself. And it cannot be said that this was due to the superior intellectual development of Polish workmen in comparison with Russian. Not at all. I speak not of peasants, but of St. Petersburg artisans, who are as intelligent as those of Warsaw. It was all due to the political antecedents of the country, to the historical tradition which every Pole seems to inherit.

We separated very late that evening, and all the town was asleep when we went out into the street. Michael accompanied me for a while. He was a great patriot, although he denied this, professing to be a cosmopolitan. But his Polish partiality manifested itself in another way—in his anxiety to prove that in every sphere of activity his compatriots were superiors to us Russians. Now he had a very good opportunity, indeed, of insisting on his favourite theme. I readily acknowledged his right to be proud of his party's achievements.

"But," I added, "it is not to yourselves that you owe the greatest part of your success."

"To whom then?"

I pointed to the ground of the long street winding before us. As there was nobody to be seen, Michael was at a loss to guess what I meant.

"You owe it, my friend, to the ground your workmen tread, to the air they breathe; that is the inspiration you have that we have not."

II.

This was the first, but by no means the last, opportunity I have had of learning what was going on in Poland. The most friendly relations between Russian and Polish revolutionists never ceased. And I will relate now in few words what I could gather about the posterior history as well as the antecedents of the new Polish revolutionary movement, of which we have had a short glimpse.

Being divided into three unequal parts between the three empires, Poland has two provinces under a constitutional *régime*, and enjoying a certain freedom of speech and of the press. Socialistic ideas had, therefore, full access to these countries, and could easily penetrate into Russian Poland, the custom-house barriers never preventing the introduction of prohibited books and papers from abroad. It is not from this side, but from the opposite one, that the new revolution infiltrated into Poland.

As is well known, a vast socialistic movement took place in Russia in 1871-3. It extended through all the land, having as chief centres the higher schools and universities. In the latter the Poles are mixing with Russian youth, and it was quite natural that the former were influenced by this strong current. The Poles proved, however, to be far less inflammable than their Russian comrades. They had a sort of preservative against the revolution in the interest of a class in the deep-rooted idea of general national revolution. The few who united in the cosmopolitan struggle of socialism took part in the Russian movement, making propaganda in Russian towns, as Drobish-Drobishevsky, and others. In 1874, however, at St. Petersburg was founded the first actual Polish circle, having for its declared purpose socialistic propaganda in Poland itself. Four Russian revolutionists formed, nevertheless, part of this circle. In 1875 they acquired many adherents in the large Polish colony of St. Petersburg; they elaborated a programme, and planned to found a paper. With these views an emissary (Mr. G——) was sent on a circular journey to Moscow, Kieff, Warsaw, and other Russian and Polish centres. In Kieff he encountered a mixed Russo-Polish self-educating socialistic circle, in which the leading spirits were Ludwig W—— and Mdlle. Plascovitzkaia, who died in 1880 in Siberia. The St. Petersburg emissary visited also the chief centres of emigration. At Lwow he saw Mr. Limanovsky, at Geneva Mr. Vroublevsky, general of the Parisian Commune, both old Polish patriots, and in London Mr. Lavrof, the editor of a Russian revolutionary periodical. All promised their assistance. Thus in the literary enterprise, as well as in the practical organisation, we see Russians and Poles united in quite a brotherly association. The publication of a paper was to be postponed, however, for some time, from scarcity of means. But the organisation grew in numbers. In the autumn of 1876 the relations with Kieff were strengthened, and two delegates were sent for permanent settlement in Warsaw. Here the St. Petersburg delegates met with Kasimir Gilt, a young man of great capacity, too early lost for his cause and his country. After being a Warsaw student, Gilt passed some years at Cracow university. Here he became an ardent disciple of the social democratic party, and, returning to Warsaw, was the chief propagator of pure scientific socialism, as formulated in Western industrial countries. His influence, due to his erudition and dialectical capacity, was very great and beneficial at the moment of creation of the young socialistic party in Poland. He neutralised the too exclusive influence of the St. Petersburg elements, educated in Russian socialistic schools, which reflected in their theoretical views the transitory social condition of Russia.

Being all members of well-to-do classes, the new socialists began by addressing themselves to their like—to students and educated people in general. The success of the new party was very great. With the speed familiar to all Polish conspiratory movements, they grew in number and extent, dividing themselves into circles, and so forth. Very soon a special group of propagandists resolved to direct their efforts to working men. In their first attempts to address workmen the propagandists adopted Russian methods of propaganda, and entered into factories as simple workmen. Thus did Ludwig W—— and two of his companions. This method was little practised in Poland afterwards, because the absence of distrust between classes made it quite useless.

For the workmen socialistic books were required. Gilt translated into Polish some pamphlets of German social democrats, as Lassalle's "Labour and Capital," and other short articles. They were printed abroad. For the propaganda among the students and educated people Russian socialistic books were used with great success. To have these supplied in sufficient quantity, the Warsaw circle, in company with the Moscow circle of Russian propagandists, organised a regular smuggling transport.

The growth of the socialistic movement in Warsaw gave rise to a similar one in Posnan and Galizia. In the latter took place, in May 1877, the first trial of Polish socialists, which was followed by many others.

From the year 1877 Warsaw became the chief camp of the new revolutionary movement. Hither converged all the forces gathered together in the principal Russian towns among Polish students. But the Poles, notwithstanding their proverbial sanguineness, showed a great sagacity by abstaining from the concentration of all disposable forces in Poland. Strong organisations were left in St. Petersburg and Kieff to get new recruits, and to maintain a reserve for every eventuality. This precaution rendered the movement considerable service, as we shall presently see.

The 8th of August, 1878, was a memorable day for the new party: the first arrest of the revolutionist of the new generation was made in Warsaw. The police discovered a printing-press, a quantity of type, some revolutionary pamphlets, and so forth. The variegated crowd assembled around the building (the arrest took place by day) was greatly excited by a sight not seen for fifteen years. An unmistakable sympathy was shown to the new victims, and when the conspirators contrived to throw from the windows some compromising papers, they were in a moment destroyed by the people before the gendarmes could come into the street to seize them.

But, anyhow, the documents which remained in the hands of the police were more than sufficient to ruin their owners, and to reveal the threads of the conspiracy. The association of Warsaw was entirely destroyed, and the remainder emigrated to Austria. There were nearly two hundred persons arrested, of whom seventy-two were accused of high treason, and twenty-four, considered as the chief instigators, condemned to severe punishments. The Government did not choose to put them on trial: this would cause too great an excitement. All was done in the administrative way, the Government having recourse to the old war commission instituted for judging the rebels of 1863, by Mouravieff, the hangman, and not abolished until recent times. Only four members of the ancient organisation remained in Warsaw; but, being obliged to conceal themselves from the police, who were at their heels, they were unable to do anything, such a comparatively small town as Warsaw not affording the facilities for the existence of outlaws like St. Petersburg.

It was just in this most critical period of the existence of the new association that its reserve, of which we have just spoken, showed its utility. Whilst the organisation made such progress at Warsaw, the organisation left at St. Petersburg and Kieff worked with the same zeal, recruiting adherents among the Poles of the respective towns. In St. Petersburg they were particularly successful. H——, and the engineer W——, its most active members, held secret meetings in the private houses of eighty to a hundred men. A secret organisation, selected with great care, was created to support the agitation. It was presided over by a central circle composed of sixteen members, and had two other auxiliary circles composed of about twenty members each. The chief purpose of the organisation was to prepare people for the propaganda in Poland. It was, therefore, essentially theoretical. Its members could not, however, abstain from taking part in the revolutionary movement of their Russian companions, which at that period began to agitate so strongly all Russian society. In great meetings, as in the startling street demonstration of the epoch, the Poles mingled with Russians. And on the editorial staff of the clandestine paper modestly called *Nachalo*, beginning which opened the series of clandestine revolutionary papers published under the very nose of the gendarmes—among the four initiators of this bold enterprise we see the engineer W——, whom I have already mentioned as one of the leaders of the Polish organisation. It was quite natural that the change which took place in the Russian revolutionary party in this period should have its influence on their Polish companions. The years 1878-9 signalise the beginning of terrorism as a practical means of struggle with the Government. But besides this practical change there was another, theoretical, known under the name of *narodnichestro*, an untranslatable word, which might be rendered by the term "peasantism," which preceded the political programme of the modern period. Its most characteristic feature is the tendency to base the revolution on the immediate desires and aspirations of the peasants. Without waiting until under the influence of propaganda, these aspirations ripen into pure socialism. Transplanted into Polish conditions, this basing the revolution on the immediate desire of the masses could mean nothing else but patriotism, nationalism, striving for political emancipation from the Muscovite yoke. All these things the Polish socialists of the first period considered as something approaching treason to their cause, which was that of cosmopolitan pure socialism. They recognised no difference between a national government and a foreign one, since both were based on the economical dependence of the working masses. It is from the year 1878-9, that the Polish socialist party in St. Petersburg made a step towards the union between socialism and nationalism. When, after the great disaster of the autumn of 1878, the delegates of St. Petersburg were called to take the place of their fallen comrades of Warsaw, the new tendencies began to take root in Poland.

But in the second period of the movement we see once more that the St. Petersburg elements find a compensation and supplement in some representatives of Western influence. Gilt was dying of consumption in Switzerland. But a little later, after the settlement of the St. Petersburg delegate, P——, at Warsaw, one of the most remarkable men of the movement, who, like many Polish patriots of past generations,—the great Traugut, for instance,— united the extreme moderation of their theoretical convictions with great ardour of temper and surprising energy in action,—P—— was quite a *white* in his theoretical opinions—a social democrat of the most moderate faction. In the capital of a conquered country he tried to introduce the pacific and nearly public methods of propaganda used in Western countries. And, thanks to his great ability and German precision in the work, as well as to the strongly marked separation of Russian and Polish elements, he succeeded in giving to the propaganda an extension which never was reached before, nor surpassed afterwards. One of P——'s adherents (Mr. B——) had even formed a bold project to turn into a public socialistic organisation the obsolete and degenerate remainders of the mediæval corporations of various trades, which had the nominal right of meeting.

The direction of this vast propagandist movement was concentrated in the hands of a secret organisation, which was, however, very simple at that time. It was divided into a central circle of organisers, composed of seventeen or eighteen people, and a number of secondary circles, which sent their delegates to the central one, and comprised some hundreds of people.

Whether it was the too large extension of the propaganda, or some chance mistake in March 1880, when the association reached the apex of its development, it was struck by the most awful disaster. The central circle was arrested to a man, so that all activity was interrupted. Once more St. Petersburg sent a supply of new forces to fill the gaps left by the fallen. But for two months nothing could be done by the St. Petersburg delegates. In June 1880, on the initiative of the St. Petersburg organisation, was convened a general meeting of the associations existing in all Russian towns. A new plan of organisation was elaborated, and many important ameliorations were introduced to render it more proof against the police. Greater circumspection was prescribed in the mode of propaganda. The organisation became more centralistic. The two large circles of organisers were replaced by a small central circle, composed of delegates from the five parts of Warsaw, with an additional bureau of representatives of student circles. In the central circle itself a division of functions between members was introduced, each having his own particular department: workmen, students, book-office, measure of general security. The growing danger of treason forced the organisation to some rigorous measures against traitors. The large workmen's circle was divided into a number of smaller ones, communicating in hierarchical order with the centres, but not with each other. All those changes proved very successful, and in the autumn of 1880—*i.e.*, only five months after the great disaster of which we have just spoken—the organisation was once more in full swing. At that time it had its ramifications in all parts of Poland, West Russia, and Lithuania, penetrating sometimes even into villages. In April 1881 it had to undergo its first serious ordeal. A refugee returning from Geneva, and entrusted with some messages to the Polish socialists, fell into the hands of the police on the frontier. Many addresses of conspirators were found among his papers. Numerous arrests followed everywhere. Treason came to augment this bad luck. About fifty persons were arrested at Warsaw, and twenty-five at St. Petersburg. Kieff, Vilna, and Belostock paid a tribute of twenty-seven victims. It was a heavy loss, but the organisation proved of good service this time by localising the damage, and preventing arrests from spreading over a large area. It was found advisable, nevertheless, to introduce further changes in the system of organisation. At that time the Russian revolutionary party of the *Narodnaia Volia*, with the celebrated executive committee at its head, in the deadly struggle of many years with all the forces of the Russian police acquired an unheard-of strength and extension. The Warsaw revolutionists adopted now the *Narodnaia Volia's* system of organisation in all its details, changing only in conformity with local conditions some particulars—as, for instance, those referring to military men. We shall abstain, of course, from describing the present organisation. It is enough to say that from that time the Polish socialist party has preserved itself from any general disaster. The arrests occurring from time to time do not involve any more the vital part of the organisation, which continues its work, gaining adherents, extending every year, having within the very limits of the Polish capital a secret printing office, which no efforts of the police can discover, and publishing a clandestine paper,— the *Proletariat*,—circulating like *Narodnaia Volia*, an achievement which was thought possible only in so large a town as St. Petersburg.

On January 29th, 1886, the young Poland had received its first christening of blood. In December of the past year twenty-nine out of hundreds of arrested were committed before the military tribunal at Warsaw—an unwonted event in the Polish capital, because formerly all political offenders were sent to Siberia without trial by administrative order. The majority—sixteen out of twenty-nine prisoners—belonged to the working classes, four of them being simple peasants. Among the remaining thirteen we see a magistrate of Warsaw, Peter Bardowsky, a man forty years old, who was one of the most daring and active members of the conspiracy; two commissioned officers, lieutenants of the Tzar's army; a captain of engineers; and half-a-dozen of well educated young university men. By the number and the social position, as well as the intrepidity of the prisoners' conduct before the tribunal, this trial was destined to be memorable in the history of the new Polish revolution. The capital punishment (the first in Poland since 1863) inflicted on four of the principal accused,—the magistrate Bardovsky, the nobleman Kounizky, and the workmen Petroussinsky and Ossovsky—has made of it an epoch in the growth of young Poland.

As to the tendencies of the organisation, the attorney's requisitory shows it to be that of "Regenerating Poland on the bases of socialism by means of the creation of a federation of self-governing communes (*gminas*) composed of working men's corporations, possessing in common all the industrial establishments as well as the land."

I will not dwell on the small divergence of theoretical opinions existing between the factions into which the Polish socialists are divided. This presents little interest for English readers. The papers, such as *Rovnost, Przedswit, Walka Klas*, all published abroad, and easily obtainable, can furnish ample materials for those anxious to know more thoroughly this subject. I will only mention that "terrorism" is introduced in the programme of the *Proletariat*. That is just the point of divergence between the two principal factions of the modern Polish socialist party—the *Proletariat* and the *Solidarity*. But if from theoretical abstractions we pass to practice, we shall see that the Polish socialists have completely abstained from such means; for the few reprisals against spies are acts of self-defence, and not of terrorism. And, if a foreigner can be allowed to speak of a country not his own, I will take the liberty of saying that I cannot see what can be the use of terrorism in such a country as Poland. As to agitating the masses, preparing them for general activity, awakening them from lethargy—nothing of the kind is wanted in Poland. For there is no lethargy in the masses of workmen, who by the former history of their country are better advanced and prepared than by any amount of terrorist attempts. More than that, many Poles who have taken part in the propaganda among Polish workmen tell that the organisers had always the greatest difficulty in keeping down their too rash temper and in moderating their desire to rush into immediate struggle. As to the political effect of terrorist attempts, everybody sees that, without doing any harm whatever to the central power, it would only give a pretext for submitting the country to reprisals, which in a conquered country like Poland may easily extend to atrocities quite impossible in Russia itself. Unless the organisation is strong enough to answer this by general insurrection, such reprisals can only increase the difficulty of any general movement.

The true service of the Polish socialist party consists in having prepared a large contingent of socialist representatives of manual as well as intellectual labour—a force which Poland did not possess in 1863. I have tried to show in a few pages what are the energy and devotion, adaptability to circumstances and self-command, of young Poland, and how she has shown herself a true and worthy successor of the old one. As to the effective results of this prolonged activity, it is far from being represented by the intermittent growth and destruction of the various clandestine organisations of which we have spoken. They are only the directing staff, and not yet the army of socialism. And in organisations carrying on this incessant battle for a new and brighter future, those who fall in largest numbers are the officers, the leaders, and not the soldiers. Those whom they lead remain for the most part. And with the intellectual and moral condition of Poland, with the surprising spirit of initiative of the working men, the impulse received is rarely lost. Poland is a fertile field for the seeds of conspiracy and subversive ideas. Thrown into the ground, they find there elements of further growth, and rarely perish. A curious instance occurred when the workmen's circles were by the disaster of 1878 cut off from communications with the centres, and were supposed to have perished. But they did not perish. They continued the work of propaganda themselves, until, in 1880, they were by chance discovered by some members of the general organisations, and united once more to the common family. In the eight years of incessant socialistic propaganda thousands of workmen in the always fluctuating population of great industrial centres have passed either through the ranks of the socialistic organisation, or sufficiently near to be influenced by the movement. And they have carried socialism everywhere. From the end of 1879 colonies of propagandists began to form in the villages, and in the winter of 1880, in the province of Kelzy, were arrested the mayor of a village commune and some peasants—the first socialists among rural classes.

Thus in the event of an insurrection Poland will have a strong contingent of socialistic elements in the field, and the longer the insurrection is postponed the greater probably will it be.

But however energetic and successful, clandestine propaganda can never extend itself over the majority of a nation. Unless we suppose the Russian autocracy will continue its disgraceful existence for many generations,—which we will by no means admit,—the coming catastrophe will find the socialist element in Poland always in a minority. This minority will have, of course, a great influence on the destiny of the country—an influence greater than in proportion to its numerical strength, as extreme parties unite together the most energetic and ardent elements. But its influence will hardly be isolated. It will have evidently to share it with old purely political parties, created during long series of generations, and not likely to lose their influence at once. The social question is complicated in Poland with national questions, as in Russia with political ones. The great advantage of Poland is, that in that country both elements have their separate representatives. The socialists can dedicate themselves exclusively to socialistic activity, as they have always done; whilst in Russia the absence of any constituted political party has thrown on the shoulders of socialists the heavy task of working as well as they can for both.

If, therefore, we want to have an idea of the

conformation of subversive forces in Poland, we must give a glance at its political parties.

III.

The epoch following the crushing of the insurrection of 1863 was the gloomiest through which the unhappy nation has ever passed.

Never were such enormous sacrifices made by a nation for the cause of its independence. There was hardly a family that had not its best men lost in the field, on the scaffold, or in the mines. All was ruin, tears, desolation. Even hope was dead. For what more could the nation do than she had done, treacherously abandoned by those who by their fallacious promises had incited and encouraged her?

If there was ever a day when the desperate cry of "Finis Poloniæ" might have escaped from a patriot's breast, it was then.

It was in those days of mourning and desolation that a voice was heard—a voice of consolation—saying, "All is not lost. We have been overpowered by the brutal physical force of the majority; but there is another force which is superior to the force of numbers—it is that of the mind. We are stronger than our conquerors by our culture, and we can use this advantage to regain what we have lost. Let us dedicate all our strength to internal development, intellectual and industrial, in order to make this difference still greater! Then we shall subdue our conqueror, compelling him to work for our welfare, and governing him whilst he thinks to govern us."

Poland has already had similar counsels, but in Velepolsky's time they were rejected as an attempt to check the revolution, growing and full of hope. Now the unfortunate country clings to them as to its last refuge. Thus was created the party of "Organic Labour," which transforms the industrial development into a political aim. This party was very strong in the first period after the insurrection, and many patriots joined it. Now the most influential of its representatives is the well-known St. Petersburg barrister, Spassovich, a Pole by origin, whose organs are the *Kray* and *Noviny*. Another of its leaders is Sventokhovsky, editor of *Pravda*. It meets with great support among the Poles who occupy the high posts in Russian civil administration. In Poland itself it is said to have degenerated into a party caring about nothing but material interests, and ready to submit to every government, provided it secures them the enjoyment of their acquired wealth. But it is undeniable that in its time it rendered considerable service to Poland. The country, weakened by so many sacrifices, wanted tranquillity and quietude, as a man after a terrible illness. And the theory of the party of "Organic Labour," like some soporific medicine, was adapted to give it some time for sleep undisturbed by phantoms and remorse. As soon as power begins to return to the exhausted body of the nation, as soon as there come into activity new generations, which feel only the wrongs inflicted by the conqueror, without having shared the ruin of hopes—

something more is required. The rich bankers may console themselves still with the fact of their superior industry, and dream themselves conquerors and masters, because they compel the Russian people of Moscow to wear their calico and their flannels. A young student, barrister, or writer cannot be so easily consoled for what is inflicted on him and his friends by Russian administrators, censors, or policemen. The bearers of the forlorn hope, the scattered mohikans of the gigantic struggle, who carry with them into remote countries the religion of the past and hope for the future, begin the work of conspiracy, and grow in strength and influence.

The prey of three rival masters, the fallacious hope of profiting by their mutual jealousy never left the Poles, however often it failed them. The State which at present can boast of the greatest sympathy among the Poles is Austria. And, indeed, the Polish provinces enjoying the greatest local liberty are surely those which fell to the share of Habsburg. Galizia has a local parliament (*seym*), much local autonomy, and no attempt is made by the heterogeneous Austrian State to keep down the Polish nationality. The traditional obscurantism of the Austrian Government alienates from it the liberal and radical parties. But all the clergy, so powerful in Poland, are heart and soul for Austria. Their chief organ is the *Czas*, of Cracow. The *Nova Reforma* and *Dzennik Polsky* are the organs of the moderate liberals, who are also in favour of Austria, believing that she is more likely to follow out the federalistic slave policy. We abstain, of course, from citing the many organs in Russian Poland that are in favour of Austria, as far as the censorship will allow them to be. The Habsburger sympathisers are said to be sufficiently numerous in Russian Poland. They are recruited chiefly from among the wealthy class; namely, those intercalated factions of that class which are not sufficiently egoistic to accept prosperity under the Tzar's sway, nor bold enough to think of open insurrection.

Whatever may be the result, the advantages and disadvantages, of the union of Poland under Austrian dominion, it is hardly necessary to say that such a dream is completely unreliable. Austria is too feeble to tear from the claws of the Russian bear the Polish provinces, and to checkmate its powerful northern neighbour. Only Germany is a serious competitor with Russia, and surely no provinces of of the Tzar's empire excite so much the insatiable appetite of the German Chancellor as Poland. In the autumn of 1883, when war between Russia and Germany was in the air, the first thing on which Prince Bismarck kept his eye was the securing the sympathy of Poland. I have it from three independent and trustworthy sources that the German Chancellor made overtures to many Polish patriots and leaders of the last insurrection, proposing to them to enter the Prussian army as officers on advantageous terms, and enticing them by prospects of the creation of a Polish kingdom with the King of Saxony at its head. It is quite beyond doubt that Poland is much more coveted by Prussia than the so-called German or Baltic provinces. The latter are much poorer, and can add little to the power of the German Empire, whilst the possession of Poland gives an excellent strategical and economical position. Besides, we must point out the fact that German colonisation was so extensive during the last generation that now the number of Germans is greater in Poland than in the Baltic provinces. The fact is surprising, but perfectly true. The reader may find it in the geography of Elisée Réclus, in the chapter on Poland. Thus if we bear in mind the definition given by Bismarck, that Germany comprises all the lands where the German language is spoken, Poland is much more Germany now than the Baltic provinces, the dominions of the old Teutonic order. In the event of a war with Russia, nothing is more likely than the realisation of such a dream. But we have every reason to think that there are few Poles who ever cherished such ideas, and who would rejoice on its realisation.

Poland hates the Muscovite yoke, wants to be free, and will be free sooner or later; but it will not be with the idea of subjecting itself to Germany. If we compare the dominions of the two states, we find, of course, that the Prussian is more tolerant from a political point of view than the Russian. There is, however, one point of great difference. Both governments are doing their best to destroy the Polish nationality, and the Russian Government is even more violent and barbarous in this point than the Prussian. But with all their goodwill the Russian Government cannot and never will be able to destroy the Polish nationality, for one simple and sufficient reason,—the superiority of Polish culture. Russian colonisation in Poland is quite impossible; the peasants and workmen would die in the competition with more skilful Poles. The Russificating element consists only of Russian tchinovniks, and a heap of swindlers and speculators attracted by the great pecuniary advantages and facilities afforded to them for acquiring lands confiscated from the patriots. Such elements are of too low a quality to have the smallest influence on the highly civilised Polish elements. All the Russificatory measures of the Government do, is to mantain unquenched the burning national hatred of its dominion.

With Germany it is quite the reverse. Here the chief factor of denationalisation is a large and various colonisation of peasants, artisans, men of the liberal professions coming from the over-populated German country. Strong by their intellectual development and workmanship, and the feeling of their nationality, this flow of colonists must exercise quite another effect, supported, as it is, by the arbitrary and violent measures of the Government, which help its compatriot to acquire political and economical predominance; and when this is found insufficient, does not recoil before the unheard-of barbarism of summary expulsions. It is not with the prospect of destruction of their nationality by German elements that Poland will give up the considerable economical advantages of the union with Russia. The chances of military struggle and diplomatic combinations may throw the unfortunate country from the hands of one of three crowned robbers to another. But what has the nation to do with those fawning and pusillanimous "parties" who are putting the heart's hopes in the good graces of any foreign king? Only the idea of the national independence will find an echo in the soul of the masses.

It remains for us to say a few words about the latest and most important of Polish political currents, the only one which, indeed, merits attention for its ultimate influence.

The purely patriotic elements of the Polish insurrection are now represented by the well-known Ej (Mialkovsky), novelist of repute and warrior. They remain quite at the same point as the insurrection of 1863 left them. A new insurrection of the same kind will put all things right. That of 1863 was unsuccessful only from some lack of prevision on the part of the leaders. The supply of arms was not sufficient. Had it been sufficient, the insurrection of 1863 would have had quite another end.

There are three points which may be urged by the friends and sympathisers of Polish insurrection. The upper and rich classes being in 1863 one heart and soul with the working classes, how can it happen that a new insurrection will be better provided with funds now, when a considerable number of the industrial class are against the insurrection, preferring the " pacific conquest" of Russia by means of cotton and woollen wares?

Much more striking are the reasons for the non-success of the Polish insurrection pointed out by more impartial observers. Eyewitnesses affirm that in great part this was due to the attitude of the peasants. Whilst the workmen of the towns were always the most ardent patriots, the peasants were often indifferent, or mostly hostile to the insurrection of the "nobles," because the Russian Government hastened to make very democratic agrarian reforms, all in favour of the masses of the peasants. Now these reforms being already introduced, will the insurrection make any new concession to interest the peasants in its success? The patriots who kept uncontaminated their political faith of 1863, gave a peremptory answer: No new concessions are to be made for the material welfare of the masses. The new insurrections, stronger than that of 1863, must be made out of pure patriotism.

As sympathisers with the Polish insurrection, we may hope that this too Roman firmness will not be maintained. The presence and growing strength of the socialist party will force the patriots to great concession, in order to secure its powerful assistance.

With the other reef of the last insurrection—the question of nationalists—the solution is not so obvious. There are two kinds of Polands: the real one, or the ethnographical Poland, where the Polish tongue is spoken by the masses, and the historical Poland, which comprises a good many provinces more, not Polish at all, and sometimes professing the deepest hatred to Polish dominion, as, for instance, the Ruthenist orthodox provinces, which formed also part of the ancient conquering Poland. It is known that the insurrection of 1863, made in the name of the historical Poland, encountered the most cruel reprisals on the part of the Ruthenian peasants, whom it wanted to liberate from the Muscovite yoke.

Now, do the Polish patriots persevere in their dream

of historical Poland? There can be no positive answer to this question, the statements of the democrats of the old school differing on this point.

But if even we suppose the best of all possible eventualities on every point; namely, that the insurrection will not have on its hands new enemies in the person of hostile peasants of the orthodox religion; that the presence of the socialist party will enforce truly democratic concessions, which will augment the sympathies of the agricultural classes—even in this case it would be a miracle that so small a country will not be crushed by the overwhelming power of the Tzar; especially now, when the concentration of so many railway lines converging towards Poland renders it quite easy to concentrate there in a few weeks 100,000 soldiers. It is quite evident that without an internal diversion, which will keep occupied the forces of the Government elsewhere, a successful rising in Poland is a chimera.

The Russian revolutionary movement, which gave so much trouble to the Tzar, could not fail to attract the attention and the sympathy of the Poles. The best mutual relations were established between these natural allies. I have already spoken of the socialists, and need not return to the subject. It is just the same with all the subversive parties of Poland; the mutual advantage and the necessity of mutual support are too evident. The difference between patriots and socialists consists in the fact that the former do not want to make propaganda of their ideas in time of peace, as the latter are doing. An insurrection for independence is preparing itself in Poland. The first signal will suffice to raise in arms its intrepid workmen. And I am able to state that the late religious and national persecution, the forced conversion of uniats to orthodoxy, suggested by the antediluvian obscurantism of people like Pobedonostzev and Tolstoi, have secured to the insurrection a much wider sympathy than it could have had otherwise.

The police have never as yet discovered patriotic conspiracies; for the patriots do not conspire, confining their attention to keeping an eye on those who may be used at an emergency. Why should they waste their strength in conspiring when, in a favourable opportunity influencing the national spirit, an insurrection in Poland may be raised in a few weeks?

Under these conditions the expectant position maintained by the Polish insurrectionary party is quite rational. Poland can be free only along with the whole of Russia. A premature insurrection would expose Poland to unavoidable ruin, and greatly impair the chances of Russian revolution in general. Poland, in the whole scheme of the movement, is what the old guard of Napoleon was in his battles. All the other forces must begin, certain that the help of Poland will not fail at the most decisive moment.

These respective positions in the day of future reckoning impose on both parties mutual obligations in the present. The union with Russian revolutionary elements imposes, as a condition *sine quâ non*, the forsaking of mediæval dreams of historical Poland, which was as aggressive a state and as regardless of the rights of nations as the Russia of to-day. On the other hand, the presence of Polish elements reacts on the Russian revolution, imposing also as a condition *sine quâ non* the acceptance of the completely federalistic idea. Poland will never accept a *régime* which does not give it full autonomy. And this once recognised for Poland can by no means be denied to any nationality entering into the present Russian Empire.

IV.

TERRORISM IN RUSSIA AND TERRORISM IN EUROPE.

TERRORISM IN RUSSIA AND TERRORISM IN EUROPE.

I.

TIME was when dynamite seemed likely to remain the exclusive patrimony of Russian revolutionists—that is to say, of Nihilists—and to have no function outside the Muscovite Empire, except the innocent industrial one of exploding mines. But in the last year events have occurred, now in one place, and now in another, which make this supposition questionable. In France, in Belgium, in Spain, in Italy, and even in England, there have been explosions of dynamite, of which the aim has been by no means industrial. It is true that the acts of terrorism committed in Europe have not as yet assumed a serious aspect, owing to the manifest want of organisation in their preparation, the inexperience shown in their execution, and the defect of concerted plan by which they are all characterised. They are all isolated attempts, evidently conceived and carried out either by single individuals or by small groups, and may be regarded as experiments in the use of dynamite rather than as political acts.

But may not this aspect of the matter change with time? The first step has been achieved, and it involves much: to the acts mentioned above, the significance of a policy has been given; dynamite has become the accredited symbol of anarchy, the banner of the extreme revolutionary party. And for a certain class of minds extreme parties will always have peculiar attractions. Will it not be possible for all revolutionary spirits who have resorted to courses of destruction and violence to unite themselves under this banner in a single organisation of a prudent and far-seeing character, which shall give a terrible concentration to these hitherto disconnected acts? It is not necessary to look far in order to find the country in which all this has already happened. The spectre of Russian terrorism rises before eyes dilated with panic, and forces upon us the question—Are the bombs and explosives of the European terrorists merely extravagances of a few hot heads, or are we on the eve of a new era in the revolutionary movement? In order to answer this question, and, what is more important, to put the reader in a position to answer it for himself, we propose to pass in review the causes of Russian terrorism—considering them impartially and as far as possible objectively, not as a political tendency, but as historical facts, the inevitable and fatal result of special circumstances, by studying which we may perhaps come to understand the conditions of terrorism in general, and so qualify ourselves to form an opinion upon the terrorism of the present anarchy.

II.

That which surprises and perplexes all those who interest themselves in the so-called Nihilists, is the incomprehensible contrast between their terrible and sanguinary methods and their humane and enlightened ideals of social progress—a contrast that is suggested most forcibly by their personal qualities. For whenever these men come actually before the eyes of the public, every unprejudiced and independent observer is forced to recognise that, instead of the ferocious monsters their acts would suggest, they are in fact men of the gentlest disposition, evidently inspired by unselfish love for their country, and, more often than not, well-educated, refined, and belonging to the best society. How is it then that men of this sort not only commit so many deeds of blood, but defend them, and proclaim them openly as fair means of political warfare?

This is the peremptory question that every historian of the revolutionary movement in Russia has to answer. And accordingly each one in turn first approaches the phenomena of terrorism from a psychological point of view, and shows how this apparent contradiction is explained by the conduct of the Government towards the socialists. On this point it may be said that there is but one opinion among competent judges.

When a Government considers all things permitted against a particular section of its subjects, and hunts them down like wild beasts, without mercy and without truce, the persecuted body are *ipso facto* absolved from all civil obligations. The social pact ceases to exist for them, and unable to put themselves under the protection of the civil law, they are constrained to appeal to the natural instinct of self-defence and retaliation, which, under the name of lynch law, prevails in the forests of the New World, where there are neither judges nor tribunals—as, in Russia, there are none for the socialists.

It is, however, a mistake to treat the ferocity of the system of repression as the sole or even the principal cause of terrorism in Russia. The acts we are considering have never been mere measures of personal defence or vengeance—they have always contained an element of aggression, of war; they have had a general purpose; they represent, in short, a *system of political strife*. And as such they have been adopted; by which I mean, that in the present condition of Russian affairs it is hoped, by these means, to realise approximately, if not entirely, the common aim of the party—that is to say, the liberty of the country.

Liberty won by assassination! exclaim the good people. The phrase has an ugly sound. We are the first to acknowledge it and to regret it. But is the idea altogether new? Is not Timoleon, the liberator of Syracuse, universally celebrated as a hero, though he slew his own brother to deliver his country from a tyrant? The executions of Charles I. in England and of Louis XVI. in France, were they not called legal assassinations by Royalists? And were they not really such? Yet who can deny that these acts helped the cause of liberty in the countries in which they were perpetrated? Why then should not the assassination of Alexander II. prove equally useful? But let us not involve ourselves in moral considerations. It is not the apology for terrorism that we are making, but the analysis of it. The task before us is to inquire rather than to palliate.

The anomaly presented by the struggle for liberty in Russia is but a reflection of the anomalies inherent in the social condition of the country.

In other countries which have had a genuine national culture liberal ideas have been developed concurrently with the material and intellectual development of the classes that stand in need of them, and the result has been the overthrow of the autocracy by the revolutionary movement; the *bourgeoisie*, valuing itself upon its influence with the working class, and especially with the more intelligent and excitable operatives of the towns, has stirred up the people to overthrow the *ancien régime*, and establish upon its ruins the parliamentary institutions that belong to the new political order. But in Russia nothing of this sort is possible. The whole nation languishes under its barbarous and incapable Government, and the agricultural class suffers most of all. Political freedom will be of the utmost benefit to the peasants, by enabling them to realise the agrarian reforms which they foolishly expect to be made by the Tzar. But this they do not understand. And the class which has to strive for political freedom is that to which it is a boon and necessity in itself—the educated class, called in Russia the intelligent class. It has, as mentioned above, no distinctive origin or even position, except such as comes by professional occupation. It includes the nobility and the educated part of the *bourgeoisie*, sons of the Church, as well as officers of the Government. It is upon this class, nourished from childhood on the liberal thoughts of the best European thinkers, and permeated by the most advanced democratic ideas, that the actual despotism presses most painfully. But with a cruel irony this class is deprived of its natural support by its moral alienation from the people, due partly to the exotic character of Russian culture, but chiefly to the fact that until 1861 the only cultured class was the slave-owning nobility. The Russian could not forgive the sons for the crimes and oppression of the fathers. A genuine Russian peasant, unless he has spent much time in town, and become educated to a better feeling, is extremely diffident, and suspicious of all those who wear a German overcoat; in other words, are connected in any way with the class to which his former masters and tyrants belonged. When in 1870 the enthusiastic rush of intelligent youths towards the people took place, only a few of the apostles of the new doctrine succeeded in making themselves acceptable to the peasants, and those had to cope with obstacles and difficulties entirely unknown and hardly imaginable to democrats of Western countries.

This social chasm is the supreme misfortune of our country. Left to itself, without means of enlightenment, the people is given over to mediæval prejudices in politics and religion, and becomes the docile and unconscious instrument by which the Government maintains the very *régime* under which the peasants suffer; while the cultivated classes, deprived of support, are placed in a truly desperate position. In their own country, surrounded by compatriots in speech and in blood, their condition is that of a race numerically small but of superior culture, subject to conquering barbarians.

This, then, is the anomaly in the social state that produces the anomaly of the political issue. There was only one course by which it could have been obviated—that the Government, accepting the situation, should have voluntarily abstained from using the material forces at command to oppress this new nation within the nation that has been begotten by the ardour of the Western breeze on the plains of the Muscovite Empire. The part of a generous conqueror would have been to recognise that this new nation had its needs and its sacred rights, however incapable it might be of asserting them by force. But this the Government has never done, and in truth cannot do, without renouncing the autocracy. It has gone to the opposite extreme, and treated the new class with a brutality rather Vandal than European. Every manifestation, however slight, of that independence of spirit which is the very breath of life to intelligent citizens—every freedom of thought or of speech it has been the policy of the Government to requite with exile or the galleys. Rebellion was inevitable, and we have it in fact. Turn Nature out by the door and she comes back through the window. Intellectual Russia was indeed unable to resort to open rebellion. It had to bear in slavish submission everything that the brutal despotism of the Tzar's bureaucracy chose to impress upon it. But they are men with blood in their veins after all, our educated classes. Offences not avenged are not forgiven; hatred concealed is not quenched. The more the nation was cowed by secular submission the greater must have been the fascination of the dashing courage and carelessness of personal danger in those who dared to provoke openly the dreaded, all-crushing power. Thus intelligent Russia, expecting to become an insurrectionary force itself, becomes in the meantime an excellent *milieu*, in which the few practical rebels found enthusiastic encouragement, moral support, material assistance, warm and safe refuge in moments of danger. For in this class there is no disposition to be squeamish about the means resorted to by the more desperate spirits; the inequality of the forces pitted one against the other is so well appreciated—the wrongs, the griefs, the outrages are so intimately felt—that everything is justified, everything applauded, provided the blow strikes to the heart of the enemy, and the serpent that strangles the whole nation is made to writhe.

These are, in our opinion, the principal causes which have led, among us, to the system of war known by the name of terrorism. The repressive measures of the Government do but supply the kindling spark: they educate socialists in the implacable hatred of oppressors, and they determine the first acts of terrorism, but they do not create terrorism: without the creation of the *milieu*, so brimful with sufferings and hatred, already indicated, these manifestations would remain isolated acts of self-defence and vengeance, and could never achieve the importance belonging to the systematised policy of a whole party. On the other hand—supposing for a moment that an impossibility had occurred—that the actual Autocratic Government, while continuing to oppress the country, had treated the socialist party with the utmost mildness; we still think it more than probable that terrorism would none the less have made its appearance in Russia—with only this difference, that in that case the movement would have begun at the point of aggression—that is to say, at *Tzaricide*—instead of passing through the preliminary phase of attacks upon Government *employés*, all acts of this character having been directly provoked by the repressive measures. In the short history of our revolutionary movement, there is an interesting incident that justifies this assumption. Karakozoff's attempt, made in 1866, was determined simply by the general policy of reaction pursued by the Government, and had no pretext of provocation in measures of repression against the socialists, who indeed hardly existed as a party at that date. We have it on the authority of one of the old members of the conspiracy that the society of which Karakozoff was a member had deliberately planned a series of similar attempts. But the times were not then mature; neither the society nor the revolutionary party was equal to so great a cause. How they have become so since, we shall see in the next chapter. Let us conclude this one with a recognition that, with the existing constitution of parties in Russia, only two courses of events are possible—either political terrorism on all sides, or a social revolution of the starving and desperate masses of the population. There is only one way of escape from this dilemma —that the revolution shall convert an integral part of the Government, that is to say, of the army, of the ministry, of the Imperial family itself, and the officials nearest to the throne. By this means the Government would be divided against itself, and the autocracy would fall to pieces by a process of natural decay. Such an event is anomalous, but the system now obtaining in Russia is an anachronism monstrous enough to make such anomalies possible. Should this state of things be realised, we should have a series of *coups d'état* and military insurrections, with more or less intervention on the part of other sections of the social body. And this is precisely the programme adopted by the party of *Narodnaia Volia*, and which they are seeking to carry out. If they succeed, it will be well for us; if not, we shall have very likely terrorism once again.

III.

In the preceding chapter we have endeavoured to point out the method and the causes of the creation of terrorism, as an idea, a tendency, and a system. We have now to consider its machinery; and on this aspect of the matter we propose to linger a little as that which is above all interesting. Modern social science teaches us that every phenomenon of social life has its material substratum, with which it is so intimately and essentially connected that it cannot exist independently of it. We shall see that this principle holds in the present case; and in order to make the application plain we will venture upon a parallel. Karl Marx, the founder of the new school of political economy, has proved to demonstration that in the course of history the creation of capital and the development of the power of the third estate, or *bourgeoisie*, has always been based upon the spoliation of peasants and artisans, and the conversion of the whole labouring class into a proletariate without property in the soil, and obliged to hire itself out for daily wages to landlords and capitalists. In like manner it may be said that terrorism is based upon the creation of a political proletariat consisting of the so-called "illegal men" or outlaws of Russian society. I have explained elsewhere that this name is given to all those who continue to live in open defiance of the police by means of false names and passports. This is a class that exists in no other country, but is numerous in Russia, in consequence of the arbitrary action of one party and the revolutionary temper of another.

The fact is that in Russia every one who has the misfortune to fall into the hands of the police as a political offender—no matter how trivial his offence may be—is, in ninety-nine cases out of a hundred, a lost man. The preliminary detention is made at the arbitrary pleasure of the prosecution, which in Russia is another name for the police: they can arrest and detain whom they will. No blame attaches to a mistaken arrest: on the contrary, the more arrests the greater the merits of the prosecutor. For instance, at the time of the trial of the "hundred and ninety-three" in 1878, there were, over and above this number of the accused, about one thousand four hundred persons arrested. Of these, half were set at liberty after a few months, but the remainder were kept in prison from one to the four years that the case lasted ; save only seventy-five, who died, some by suicide, some of consumption, some insane. And in more recent times, when the white terror followed upon outbreaks of revolutionary terrorism, and especially in the reign of Alexander III.,—who invented a species of political proconsuls, such as Strelnikoff, to devastate towns and provinces, and arrest right and left,—the severities have been even greater. But I have no positive figures at hand.

The normal penalties for political crimes are simply Draconian—ten years at the galleys for a single speech, or for reading or preserving a proclamation. And whenever a prosecution follows an outbreak, the tribunal receives special orders to aggravate the penalties so as to make "a salutary example," and the verdicts become legal assassinations of the most monstrous character. The lad Rosovsky was condemned to death, and actually hanged at Kieff on the 5th of March, 1880, for merely having in his house a proclamation of the Executive Committee. The same judgment was passed on the student Efremoff for having lent a room in his house to two revolutionists who were concerting a plan of escape without even taking their young host into confidence. But his sentence was commuted to a lifelong condemnation to the galleys, in consequence of his having made an appeal for mercy. Drobiasgin, Maidansky, Lisogub, Tchubarov, were all hanged—some for having subscribed money to the revolutionary cause, others for conveying a box, of which they did not know the contents: offences, one and all, which the actual law of the country punishes only with exile or a few years of imprisonment.

But is there not a degree of innocence that can avail even before a Russian tribunal? If a man knows himself to be absolutely uncompromised in any revolutionary enterprise; if the police, on searching his house, could find, no compromising document; if no treacherous deposition aggravate his danger,—might not this man hope to get off with a few months, or at the utmost one, two, or three years of detention, and be left in peace for the rest of his life, with health impaired, perhaps, but not ruined, a future spoiled but not destroyed, and the means of recovery with time and industry? Even so poor a hope as this will prove illusory in Russia. The principle of the terrible *law of suspects* is that not only the act, but the thought and the intention shall be punished, and that these can be divined by the intuition of *clairvoyant* policemen, who need no proofs to confirm their guesses. It is an altogether exceptional and astounding thing for a man once implicated in a state prosecution to be ever again left in peace. Convicts with definitive sentences, just after they have served out their term of punishment, as well as those who are acquitted by the tribunals, even the very witnesses (who had also suffered imprisonment to make them more malleable), except, of course, those on the side of the prosecution, are generally sent afterwards into exile by *order of the administration*. The imposition of this final penalty is left entirely to the discretion of the police, who are guided only by information privately received, and who, according to the behaviour of the witness or implicated person before the tribunal or the judge, pronounce sentence of exile and appoint the place of punishment. This last point is a very weighty one, for it makes a material difference to a man whether he is sent to the uttermost parts of Siberia or to some less remote region. It is, moreover, in the power of the police to extend or shorten the term of exile at their pleasure. But they are in little haste to shorten it. Without any exaggeration, we may declare that no man of the opposition who refuses to renounce his convictions, or to pretend hypocritically to do so, will ever be recalled from exile, even though he may have committed absolutely no offence. Some of the witnesses in the case of Netchaieff, tried in 1871, are to this day in administrative exile.

And what is this administrative exile? A horrible slow decay, an undermining of the whole moral and physical constitution of a man, a consumption by slow fire. We need not speak of administrative exile in Eastern Siberia, among the wild Yakut of the horrible deserts, in the country where winter lasts ten months and cold reaches to 40 or 50 degrees below zero; where no clothing can be had but untanned skins of beasts, where bread is a rare delicacy, and almost the only luxury is a meal of rotten fish; where there are no human beings to exchange speech with, for the aborigines speak an unintelligible gibberish; where the post comes but once in the year. In these icy deserts exile is worse than the galleys. Nevertheless, it is inflicted *administratively* that is to say, at the sole will and pleasure of the police, and for offences too trivial (when not purely imaginary) to be cited even before a Russian tribunal.

But enough of this. Let us consider administrative exile in its milder forms—in Western Siberia or Northern Russia. Here we are in civilized countries—at least so far as the material side of life is concerned. There are houses to live in, there is food to eat, the European costume is in vogue. Only in order to enjoy all this we must have money or the means of earning it. But how shall this last be done without intercourse with other citizens? And this is just what the Government is determined to prevent, on the ground that "loyal subjects" are in danger of being corrupted. Hence the monstrous regulation of March 12th, 1882. It is forbidden to administrative exiles to give lessons, or occupy themselves in any educational function, or even to give instruction in manual arts. They are also forbidden to hold conferences, to take part in scientific meetings, or to attend theatrical performances, to serve in libraries, in printing offices, in lithographers' or photographers' shops, or even as journeymen labourers; and always for the same reason—to obviate the risk of propaganda. On the same ground those who are doctors, chemists, or accoucheurs, are forbidden to exercise their respective professions. Finally, because many of them are men of letters, they are forbidden to contribute to reviews and newspapers (§§ 24th, 27th). What means of earning their bread is left to them? Manual labour, in some cases. But what does that mean for educated men who have never held a workman's tool in their hands? And even that is not always permitted. The Government does not think itself safe, short of granting discretionary power to the administration, to forbid any exile to practise his own handicraft (§ 28th).

Obviously, having thus deprived the exiles of the means of earning their living, it is incumbent upon the Government to maintain them, like prisoners, at the public cost. And in fact this obligation is recognised in principle, and a monthly allowance is made to every political exile—eight roubles to those who are of noble origin, and four to those who are not noble. The larger sum is about equal to sixteen shillings, the smaller to eight shillings, a month. Such an allowance as this is a mockery. And were it not for the contributions of friends and relations, which all the exiles share like brothers, they must all die of starvation. But the friends of the exiles are overburdened with other expenses; and the utmost they can do for their unfortunate comrades amounts to little more than a few crumbs cast into an abyss of indigence. The exiles sink into a state of squalid misery, and their health wastes away for want of the commonest necessaries of life. At the same time, the absence of books and newspapers, the want of occupation and of intellectual interests, in this death-in-life, dragged out from day to day under the incessant *espionage* of the superintendents, produces a dull despair and apathy that wears out the spirit even more terribly than the physical hardships ruin the body. Those who have suffered it for a few years feel the effects of it all their lives, and maintain that even the misery of solitary confinement is preferable to this slow consumption prolonged through years and years, and sometimes through a lifetime. Proof of this lies in the number of suicides that occur among the administrative exiles.

Such is the future that awaits not only every revolutionist in Russia, but every member of the opposition who has once come in contact with the police. It would be easy to fill whole pages with examples of arbitrary inflictions of the extreme penalty. Not seldom, the police are unable to formulate any kind of definite accusation, and the charges written against the names of men sent to perish in Siberia will be of this sort—"he belongs to a dangerous family," "has perverse opinions," "had a brother who was hanged!" We have not as yet complete statistics as to these exiles. It is, however, calculated approximately that in the reign of the two Alexanders their number amounted to five or six thousand—the flower of a whole generation brought to the sickle like the corn in ear. Verily, in these scattered hamlets of the desert, the youth of Russia is immolated. It is not necessary to seek further for the causes of sterility in all our fields of intellectual labour; a country as poor as ours in intellectual resources cannot stand this constant letting of its best blood.

But now let us suppose the case of a man who, by some lucky chance, learns beforehand that he is regarded with suspicion by the police. An inquiry, followed by an arrest, is inevitable. Beyond this, the event is doubtful: he will be cited to a trial of some sort, and may appear either at the prisoner's bar or in the witness box; he may be acquitted or condemned, hanged or restored to provisional liberty. All these points are uncertain, and a man of sanguine temperament may flatter himself that the issue is doubtful also; but, in fact, one thing is certain, he will be sent into administrative exile, and will suffer all its miseries; and unless he is prepared to be a hypocrite, or to make compromises, he must lay his account to spending the best years of his life in such exile, if not to die in it. Unless, indeed, he will have recourse to the only remaining expedient—flight.

In this case, is it not better to fly at once?

Accordingly, he flies. All who hold the revolutionary faith fly; those only who have not sufficient faith to endure the life of an outlaw remain, because their position in the heart of the revolutionary movement would be like that of an atheist priest within the Church.

It is precisely the predominance of the revolutionary faith that has created this class of outlaws. In former days a man being warned that he was compromised with the Government, began by getting out of the way, and kept in hiding until he could succeed in crossing the frontier; then he devoted himself either to active agitation among the European populations, or to the literary propaganda of revolutionary ideas. But since the year 1873, when the movement reached its maturity, and was reinforced by new life and ardour, to abandon one's country and agitate abroad has been felt to be too painful a course, and the resolution has been taken to remain on the soil and work for the cause under cover of false passports. At this point the new figure of the "illegal man" comes into the political field.

We have seen that the anticipated arrest is the

principal means of his creation. Such cases occur every day; never an arrest takes place that does not carry with it *loss of legality* (as the Nihilist phrase has it) for several citizens, whose addresses, letters, or photographs show them to be friends or acquaintances of the accused; the most energetic of these always resort to outlawry, and their number is swollen by those who, less fortunate or less resolute, have not been able to evade arrest, and after being sent into exile, contrive to get away from their station, a comparatively easy matter. And, finally, these are joined by a curious contingent of *volunteer outlaws*, consisting of men who renounce legality before they have even compromised themselves, knowing well that they stand in daily risk of doing so, and not wishing to be caught unprepared. Such are the sources from which *illegal Russia* has sprung into existence. Statistics are wanting by which to estimate its numerical strength; we can only say that it is less than it should be in the present condition of Russia; and this because none enter into it except the socialists. Even so, however, the number of "illegal men" who have come upon the scene must be reckoned by hundreds.

These outlaws may be described as men deprived of all political and civil rights. If they have had a profession, a trade, or any sort of occupation, they can no longer practise it, for to make themselves known is to be arrested. If they are men of property, they must renounce all rights of property; for having lost their identity, they are no longer in a position to enjoy their estates, or to alienate them by will or gift. If they have families, they must disown them, for they cannot venture to see them any more. The police, knowing the weakness of human nature, keeps special watch over the near relations of every "illegal man," and seizes the opportunity of a stolen interview to effect his arrest. His sweetheart will sometimes follow him, abandoning everything for his sake.

All these things taken into consideration, the position of the "illegal man" is not so miserable or so defenceless as might be supposed. For these reasons. Their own number is considerable, and the number of those who, without throwing in their lot with them, are yet willing to help them, is simply enormous. So that they constitute a State within the State, having their own organization, their particular code of manners and customs, an independent public opinion, a special press and various offices of government, among which the most important are the passport office and the finance office—by which the community provides for the needs of its members. This mysterious republic, in constant war with the Government, is moreover on terms of peace and amity with all the world outside. Altogether the life of such an outlaw is as different as possible from what a European reader might suppose, if he judged by the case of man in a corresponding position in any other country. The Russian outlaw is on his guard, but he is not obliged to hide himself. He goes about openly, frequents public haunts and domestic circles, attends theatres and concerts, becomes a member of scientific and literary societies, etc., etc.; and wherever he goes he meets people who are aware of his *illegality*.

But he has nothing to fear from them, for any one who should betray his secret would incur universal contempt, and be counted irredeemably dishonoured for the rest of his life. Generally speaking, it may be said that an "illegal man" stands in no danger whatever so long as he keeps quiet. The real and only danger is when he puts himself in relation with comrades to concert a revolutionary attempt.

It is from among this class of "illegal men" that the ranks of terrorism are recruited, and I affirm that the creation of this class of men, destitute of political rights, and outlawed, is the *conditio sine quâ non* of the creation of terrorism as a system. The one is the material substratum of the other. The truth of this assertion may be tested by a single question. Is it possible to carry on an organised revolutionary movement in the manner of Zassoulitch—that is to say, can every man who takes part in a revolutionary act consign himself afterwards into the hands of so-called justice, as Vèra Zassoulitch did when she shot General Trepoff? This is a question that admits of no answer but a unanimous and emphatic "No;" except perhaps on the part of mere lookers-on, quiet citizens who, knowing nothing of the real working of revolutions, always imagine the revolutionist to be an abnormal creature outside the ordinary laws of human nature. The revolutionists of all countries, and especially those of Russia, will answer with one accord that on these terms a systematic revolution is a thing absolutely impossible; no party, however enthusiastic, *exalté*, heroic, can produce men like Zassoulitch by the dozen.

But the violence of the Russian despotism has created the class of "illegal men," and so solved the problem. The revolutionary outlaws are men sacrificed in advance. They know that the fatal hour must come for each one of them sooner or later; and one and all they throw themselves into the desperate struggle initiated by a handful of heroes. I do not know who it was that calculated the average duration of an "illegal man's" life at two years. Possibly the estimate is even too long. But in that short space there is no definite moment or act that is known beforehand to be the fatal one —an important point, as every one knows who understands human nature. The outlaw knows that he stakes his life upon every enterprise in which he embarks, but he knows also that by courage, resolution, and presence of mind he may escape death, and that in that case he loses nothing, while he gains the satisfaction of having done his duty well. It matters little to him that the police are on his track; he is not a person—but a shadow, a number, a mark. He has but to change his name, his passport, and his dwelling-place, and he vanishes, to begin life anew. If through any unfortunate combination of circumstances his real name transpires, he only suffers the annoyance of being, for a short time, carefully sought by the police. Protected and hidden in his little world beyond the law, he can afford to laugh at their pains; and, after a short interval of repose, he appears again and once more openly defies the emeny. Neither does he lose consideration in general society if he has any relations there which he cares to maintain; for the devotion and affection of "loyal subjects" to their Tzar is of such a singular character that a man who has attempted the life of his sovereign, or of one of his ministers, does not thereby lose respect and esteem, or cease to be a welcome guest in the houses of the best society. (This is a statement that will provoke a shriek of rage from Katkoff, the present vice-emperor; but neither he nor the Government can deny its perfect truthfulness.) Least of all does the prospect of punishment deter the "illegal man" from attempting desperate deeds. That is a consideration that does not weigh with him for a moment; he knows that as a revolutionist he has no hope of escaping, whatever he does or does not do. He is only concerned to crowd into the brief term of life allotted to him the greatest possible number of services to the cause of liberty and of injuries to the common enemy.

But the opposing forces are so unequal that the revolutionary party cannot carry on the struggle in the form of war. Its soldiers often transform themselves into voluntary martyrs, and invoke victory for their cause, after the manner of the Roman leaders, by dedicating themselves to the infernal gods. Such was the part of Solovieff, of Grinevezki, of Karakosoff, of Mlodezki, and others. But these cases of exceptional heroism, and indeed all the general heroism displayed by the revolutionary party to the amazement, and even the admiration, of their very enemies—is it not due in no inconsiderable degree to this life beyond the law and under the sword of Damocles?

We have no sympathy with the apotheosis of a

nation any more than of a party. If the Nihilists have any virtue peculiar to themselves (as they certainly have some defects) it is in consequence of the conditions in which they live. The ancients said: *poetæ nascuntur oratores fiunt*. We may say with more truth that heroes are not born, but are moulded in the school of danger and sacrifice. Man is altogether a creature of habit. There is nothing to which he may not be accustomed: to privations and inconveniences, to things pleasant as well as unpleasant. By merely having it every day and each day before his eyes, he may become so used to danger that he will not think of it. He may become indifferent even to the idea of death, by looking it constantly in the face and carrying it always in his thoughts. A Russian traveller relates that once, when he was visiting the monastery of Mount Athos, an earthquake occurred during the celebration of mass. All the congregation were seized with panic, and rushed out of doors shrieking. But the monks remained at their posts and went through the service with imperturbable calm. When the shock was over, the traveller expressed his surprise to a friend among the monks, who answered simply: "What surprises you? Is not all our life a preparation for death?" A like answer may be given by the Russian revolutionary about to ascend the gallows with a firm step. Sophie Perovskaya, a few days before her execution, wrote to her mother: "My fate does not afflict me in the least, and I shall meet it with complete tranquillity, for I have long expected it, and known that sooner or later it must come." We do not pretend, therefore, that these men are, in any sense, giants—or even strange freaks of chance or nature ; we will not even call them rare and passing types, but simply men who have been well trained in the awful school the Russian Government supports. So long as this school exists, and education in it continues to be compulsory, the supply of such people will not fail.

Those anomalous conditions which created these two constituted elements of the terrorism of 1878-81 in Russia—men disposed to fight to the last, and surroundings which enabled them to fight a considerable length of time—we consider the only ones in which similar or analogous phenomena can develop. They are natural because derived from human nature. Everything has its limits. The spirit of self-sacrifice for what it thought right is like everything else. It can go thus far, but not farther.

At the same time it is quite evident that the plan to be adopted, with a view to destroy and render for ever impossible the recurrence of terrorism, is the pacification of the country by the removal of the causes which created the latent discontent that makes possible such a ruthless form of internal struggle. In Russia this can be obtained by the concession of political freedom, and by no other means. Now this seems to be farther off than ever. The reaction is raging with unbounded sway. The general condition of society is more wretched and miserable than ever. Our would-be national Government is in the position of a hated conqueror, maintaining its power by main force. Arrests, banishments, summary executions,—the maintenance of the state of siege for half Russia,—are doing their work uninterruptedly. Those who are not willing to bend their heads to the yoke are virtually or politically outside the law, and constitute a tremendous stratum of explosive materials. The subversive elements are quiet for the moment. But the apparent calm is not to be trusted. Modern Russia may be compared to Germany during the Thirty Years' War, when the whole country teemed with volunteers. The cry of a popular leader and some striking examples suffice to turn them into an army, and put the country to fire and sword. What will be the form of the next outburst of revolution nobody can predict—the future will decide. Under certain circumstances the revolution may enter upon the period of open insurrection, half military, half civil, of which we have spoken in our first chapters. Under other circumstances it may throw in its lot as a powerful factor, with a still larger and more momentous movement—a general revolution of which we shall speak in our concluding pages. But in the desperate conditions in which intelligent Russia is living, with a nervously excitable people like ours, with such enormous concentration of power and responsibilities, which, like the high top of a mountain peak, attract the thunderbolt of revenge—in such a country nothing can be a guarantee against the possibility of the revolution assuming once more its acutest though narrowest form, as in the struggle of 1878-81. As things are at present nobody but a fool can feel certain as to the tranquillity of the country, any more than one can sleep peacefully in a house under which a barrel of dynamite is concealed.

IV.

I have completed my study of terrorism in Russia, and it only remains for me to come back to the question concerning the nascent terrorism in Europe, which I put at starting. Is it the beginning of a new revolutionary movement—has it a future?

I need not linger long over the answer, which the reader can hardly have failed to anticipate. I do not believe that dynamite will ever be naturalised in Europe as a political agent. I do not think that terrorism has a future there.

The situation in Russia has been determined, as we have seen, by the fact that the party through which the actual political revolution is maintained is numerically so small, that were it to venture upon an open trial of its strength, it must inevitably be overpowered by the Government, which has the mass of the people at command. In Europe, on the other hand, the revolutionary movement is not so much political as economical, and the class concerned in it is the strongest as well as the largest numerically; so much so, that a considerable section of it,—let alone the whole,—supposing it to be united and determined to act, would suffice to oblige all its enemies to lay down their arms. Therefore, for European revolutionists to make personal attacks upon the Government or the *bourgeoisie*, would be as absurd as if, in the last Franco-Prussian war, Moltke, Manteuffel, and other Prussian generals, instead of encompassing the weak enemy with their mighty battalions, would seek to penetrate in disguise to the heart of the French camp to engage in single combat with Napoleon, Bazaine, and MacMahon, instead of meeting them at the head of their battalions.* Terrorism has no *raison d'être* on European soil, and will therefore not succeed in forming for itself the indispensable surrounding of a mass of sympathisers and supporters.

Moreover, the cause wants soldiers; there are no "illegal men" in Europe like those of Russia. The conditions of European life have certainly produced revolutionists and socialists, but these are not driven to put themselves beyond the law in order to work for their ideals. They remain citizens of their respective countries, and will certainly not sacrifice willingly the possibility of appearing in public, and speaking freely and openly—the only means by which men can seriously influence their fellow-citizens in Europe.

But if the adoption of terrorism as an organised system of political warfare is absolutely impossible in Europe, what is the meaning of those acts of terrorism that occur now here, now there? We are very far from approving of them. On the first page of the number of the *Narodnaia Volia*, published shortly after the death of President Garfield, the following declaration appeared:—

"While expressing profound sympathy with the

---

* Invert the comparison and imagine that by misadventure a single company of franctireurs, left alone to defend their country against the invaders, act in the same way towards the Prussian generals—you have then the case of the Russian Nihilists.

American people in the death of President James Abram Garfield, the Executive Committee feels itself obliged to protest in the name of the Russian revolutionary party against all acts of violence like that which has been perpetrated. In a country where the liberty of the subject allows peaceful discussion of ideas, where the will of the people not only makes the law but chooses the person by whom it is administered—in such a country as this political assassination is a manifestation of the identical despotic tendency, to the destruction of which we are devoting ourselves in Russia. Despotism, whether wielded by individuals or by parties, is equally condemnable, and violence can only be justified when it is opposed to violence" (No. VI., Oct. 23rd, 1881).

This declaration sums up the feeling of Russian revolutionists in regard to the real terrorism in Europe, and we can but endorse it. Nevertheless, it would be neither very philosophical nor altogether reassuring to regard the acts of terror committed on European soil as mere manifestations of individual wickedness and madness. For what guarantee should we have against madmen? To us it seems that these acts are the fruit of class hatreds and antagonisms developed under the influence of foreign examples, and without due regard to the conditions of the struggle into a sanguinary political theory. It is precisely for this reason that we do not believe they will continue long. In politics no course is adopted without the hope that it will make its party the strongest; and the modern anarchists (we should rather say a few knots of anarchists) would not have betaken themselves to terrorism if they had not expected to draw a number of people into their camp, and inaugurate a movement of considerable importance which, for the reasons indicated above, can never be realised.

There is, however, one important factor in the problem, by means of which the life of this stillborn babe may perhaps be artificially prolonged. To wit, the action of those governments who, wishing to avoid the state of things that has come about in Russia, have had the unlucky inspiration to adopt the methods used by the Russian Government in struggling against its opponents, putting all who profess certain opinions beyond the pale of the law, and making life unbearable to them. Is not this a reproduction of Russia in miniature? But it is always the same; repression is the easiest and quickest mode of response to what Carlyle would have called a "petition of hieroglyphs." Nothing so simple as to blow brains out and refuse to inquire into anything.

What is to be done by those who will take the trouble to decipher the hieroglyphs in order to satisfy the abstruse petition it is not my business to answer. I leave it to others. As for me, I have only endeavoured to show, by a true exposition of Russian events, a useful example of *what should not be done*, of that which all civilised countries should avoid as completely as possible.

V

EUROPEAN SOCIALISM AND THE DYNAMITE EPIDEMIC.

EUROPEAN SOCIALISM AND THE DYNAMITE EPIDEMIC.

I.

THE prognostications about the inherent improbability of the vast extension and further development of "terrorism" in Europe which end the former chapter seem since to have been confirmed in the most peremptory way. The dynamite explosions which a few years ago produced in a certain part of society something almost approaching to panic, have not been heard of for a considerable length of time. The dynamite attempts, though subsiding in practice, are quite fresh in people's memory. And since there is no guarantee that under certain circumstances they cannot be repeated, it is well worth our while to investigate more closely the causes and circumstances of their origin.

I must begin a long way off, because the action and component parts of one subversive element cannot be represented in its true light without speaking of those which surround it. And I must apologise for perhaps offending some of my readers' susceptibilities in speaking of a country which is not my own.

It is a commonplace saying that ours is a time of general transformation, levelling, and rebuilding.

There is, however, a great discrepancy as to the final aim to which this reconstruction is tending. The majority, arrayed under the banners of Radical, Liberal, and other progressive parties, opine that it will be only the partial improvement of the present system, by making the laws more democratic and life more human. I adhere to the minority, who think that the general reconstruction will affect the very foundations of modern society,—*i.e.*, the economical arrangements,—and will ultimately transform the present wage workers into the proprietors of every sort of instruments of labour. This means socialism in one form or another.

Much has been spoken and written by the partisans of both systems, to show the respective advantages of the one and the disadvantages of the other. I will not repeat the arguments of those with whom I am siding. From the objective and historical point of view which I take it has comparatively little interest. Whether we like or dislike socialism, the fact is that modern Europe, with the most industrial state at its head, is unmistakably marching toward it.

The peremptory cause of it lay in the gradual democratisation of European culture, in the remarkably quick enlightenment of the working masses, in the growth of their class consciousness and capacity for organisation, as well as in the improvement of their material conditions. The opponents of socialism have given themselves much trouble to prove the latter point. If we take only the period of great industry beginning at the last quarter of the eighteenth century, there can be no doubt about it.

From 1833, and especially from 1844 and 1850, which years were marked by important Factory Acts, the conditions of workmen have wonderfully improved. As long as they are not out of employment, of course, the workmen receive higher wages and live more comfortably. But it is quite a mistake to draw from this premise a conclusion against socialism. It is not misery and degradation that give birth to social changes. Were it so the most backward and barbarous countries would have been the first in carrying out social reforms. But history shows us that the element determining the realisation of reforms is the strength and not the sufferings of those who are interested in it. Now, in the most advanced countries of both hemispheres—in England, France, Germany, and Italy, as well as in the United States of America—the working classes steadily and continually acquire a greater command over the political, intellectual, and material forces of their respective countries. And in no country has this progress been more signal than in that which in the course of only ten years introduced the School Board system, which will mark an epoch in popular education, and the Franchise Bill, which gives the virtual control of political power into the hands of the democracy—the working men of the towns and the villages. They will remould sooner or later the social and political institutions in a way that their interest may be foremost—just as the middle class did in the end of the past and first half of the present century on the Continent, when the forces of this class became equal to the task. The most important and vital interest of the working classes being with economical concerns, it is this branch that they will remould to their advantage, which in its ultimate end is nothing but socialism. And if we get rid of the narrow and purely mechanical conception of the idea of a revolution, we must acknowledge that this remoulding has already begun. The growing strength of the working classes has already manifested its influence in modifying the relations between employers and workmen, between proprietors of the instruments of work and the hands who are using it for the creation of goods. The Factory Acts, limiting the work time and regulating the work in the principal industries of this country; the Irish Land Bill of 1871, depriving the Irish landlords of a good deal of right recognised to be inherent to proprietorship—are the first attempts in this direction, feeble as yet, but unmistakable and highly important, since they admit in principle the legislative intervention in industrial concerns and with the rights of property. The extent which the agitation for the nationalisation of land has received in so short a time in England; the great stress laid on very radical economical reforms by the programmes of some of the most prominent men of the present parliament—all this shows clearly enough that the encroaching on the present economical system will not stop here. The world is going fast nowadays, and the process of social fermentation has acquired striking intensity and thoroughness. Thus the Irish question has ripened singularly in a few years, and a very radical solution of it seems to be at hand. If not settled by the Liberals to-day, it will be settled by the Radicals to-morrow. And when once settled, nobody can doubt its deep and lasting influence on the minds of the agricultural as well as industrial working men on this side of the Channel. The great demand put forward at the end of the nineteenth century: the security of man's work and man's material well-being against the caprice of the market and the will of employers, once obtained under certain obligations by the Irish tenants, cannot long be denied to the English workmen. The social revolution is in full work in England. More than ever England can be said to stand at the head of the historical development of the civilised world, leading to socialism as it formerly led to political freedom. Whether the attributing of such a part to England will be taken as very flattering by my readers, or whether they would rather prefer to be spared such a compliment, I do not know. In either case I will say that I have on my side the authority of Karl Marx, who in his preface to " Das Kapital " says that the process of the " social transformation is evident in England, so that it can almost be touched by the finger. And having arrived in England at a certain intensity, it will undoubtedly find an echo on the Continent." This was written in July 1867, and since that time the great thinker's judgment has only been confirmed.

True, there have been as yet no barricades, no bloodshed, nothing, in a word, which is usually connected with the idea of a "revolution;" and there is little probability of a similar thing being in store in the future. But this proves only that in England this revolution has found its proper and natural way of realisation. Because in what is called a "social revolution" the peacefulness of proceedings is not only a thing desirable, as in political changes, but the indispensable requisite of its fruitfulness, I may say its fulfilment. This difference is by no means an accidental one. It lies in the very nature of the transactions both the revolutions have to deal with, and I cannot put too much stress in insisting on this difference.

Economical transactions—the care for the supply of the material requisites for life—is certainly the most important function in the body social. There is hardly an individual in the community who is not affected most feelingly by any change in the domain of economical transaction, as likely to influence the amount of good he has for his share in life. And for the main mass of the community the work for material existence fills up their whole lifetime, and is almost a synonym for their life itself. Being thus the most momentous of all the interests, the economical transactions are at the same time the most delicate of all, possessing little, almost no force of resistance against the inclemency of exterior influences. The need for the consumption of all sorts of goods is too great to admit much sparing of them. The general statistics show that, contrary to the current notion, almost the whole of the yearly produce of national work is consumed in the course of the same year. In the wealthiest of European nations—the English—the total amount of centuries of accumulation makes about one and a half year's produce. England, as its statistics boast, is so rich that she could maintain her present population in idleness for full eighteen months. But if we remember that for about two centuries and a half she has had no revolution or serious internal trouble, causing great waste of property; that from the fourteenth century English industry was constantly prospering, and from 1770—the epoch of great mechanical discovery and application of machinery—it entered on a period of wonderfully rash development,—if we remember all this, the rate of accumulation will appear to us very slow indeed. It amounts to less than 1 per cent., even if we take for starting-point the beginning of the great industry, and not the great geographical discoveries of the sixteenth century. This wealth seems great only because heaped up in the hands of a very small body of people. The bulk of the nation, earning their bread in the sweat of their brows, live from hand to mouth, consuming what they earn by a week's labour during the next week, and there are few who are capable of sustaining themselves by their savings more than a fortnight or so.

Such being the case, it is only natural that the slightest change in economical conditions is instantaneously and most painfully felt by the country. The so-called commercial and industrial crises, which hardly ripple the surface of the whole momentous stream of human work, are one of the greatest disasters that a community can incur. In the present condition of nations and international industry, in which the chief branches of manufacture of the most advanced countries are calculated for export trade, a measure which should disturb the regular course of the whole of the national work only for a few weeks would produce such a general cataclysm as the world has never seen. This makes entirely impossible any sudden and violent readjustment of economical conditions. The simple approach or probability of such a measure would produce the most disastrous effect, which would prevent any possibility of its realisation. The present form of economical conditions, as created by the whole of historical influences, cannot be changed unless its substitution by a new one might be performed without any interruption or relaxation of the work ; and this can take place only if a very considerable part of the nation, virtually leading the bulk of it, has previously come to an understanding and agreed upon what is to be done in main points and in details. But in that case there is no need, and, therefore, no room, for a " revolution " in the ordinary acceptation of the word ; *i.e.*, for a violent outburst accompanied with a physical struggle. What is violence if not the effort of the weak to assert its right against the strong ? If the party aspiring, after remoulding the economical conditions of the country, embrace a very considerable minority enjoying the full confidence of the bulk of the nation, such party can realise the desirable change in an evolutionary way ; *i.e.*, with little if any violence at all, being so incomparably stronger than its adversaries.

This is, however, a mere theoretical supposition. In practice things can never come to such a sudden though pacific transformation. The fact of the possibility of the vast preparation we are speaking of implies necessarily a high standard of political freedom in the country, because without it no serious change can be wrought in the spirit of the nation. Now in a country in which the private as well as the collective initiative has full play, and the masses have control over political power, a new idea as soon as it has entered into the conception of the masses will by-and-by receive practical application, and give its stamp both to the legislature and to institutions depending on private initiative. Thus from whatever side we approach the question we arrive at the idea of the social evolution as the only possible interpretation of the may-be "revolution."

In the great complication of modern, social, and political life, in which political and economical questions are so closely united, it would be too presumptuous to expect that so arduous and burning a question as the economical one can be carried out and settled quite smoothly, without hitches or disturbances of any kind. In the countries of imperfect political freedom the governing classes, by obstinately obstructing this natural process of the introduction of new conceptions into practical life, or by interfering with the forces of the State in favour of one of the contending parties, may certainly provoke and even necessitate disturbances or even partial revolt. But such revolt can play but a secondary part in the large and organic process of social transformation by removing the obstacles to its free course. They have in them more of a political than of a social revolution. The social revolution is a task too complicated and difficult for the resources of an insurrection.

II.

If we consider the whole of the political concerns of a nation—*i.e.*, all the complex network of law, customs, written and unwritten precept of conduct regulating the relation of the individual to his fellow-citizens and to the State—we shall certainly find that they are as important by their influence on the life of the community as they are impressive by the enormous total of human work they represent. Reducing the influence of political forms to their ultimate expression, we can say that they determine whether the whole of the intellectual power the nation can produce in a given social condition is applied to the work of progress, enlightenment, and development of better forms of social life; or whether this collective intellectual power of the nation will be somewhat clipped or half suppressed, or almost entirely stifled, as is the case, for instance, in modern Russia. Viewed in this light, the influence of the political forms of a nation can hardly be exaggerated. They affect in the end not only the moral character, the intellectual development, and the culture, but even by their intermediary the material welfare of the country. The civil training or education of a nation is, however, due in very insignificant part to the real work of those who in any given moment are concerned with it, from legislators down to philosophers, poets, writers, and other teachers of the people. This is a work of all the past as well as of the present. Work in this domain produces its effect slowly, but it possesses a considerable power of perduration. We may say it is the very reverse of the work in the economical domain; its absolute amount is insignificant, but it leaves a considerable deposit, whilst the other is extremely extensive, but has almost no deposit at all.

The share of the government proper in this work of civil education is not very extensive. It maintains order and internal peace as far as it goes, which allows the other elements of society to proceed in their civilising mission, as long as they are not restricted. But the internal peace and order being maintained for long series of generations, finish by entering into people's habits and customs, and the laws are obeyed, and order preserved by its own tradition, with quite an insignificant amount of current work represented in the governing body. Thus we observe that, whilst the main mass of the community spends almost the whole of its lifetime to provide for its material existence, only an imperceptible quota of human work is spent to keep in order the political concerns of the community. In a district of 10,000 people, who are to a man engaged in a daily struggle for existence and for a better share in the enjoyment of material good, one magistrate with a few constables, one administrator with a few clerks, suffice to do all the work required for securing to the community perfect ease in carrying out their affairs. It is, of course, an important question for our small community to have these officials as wise as Solomon and as honest as Aristides. But if they happen to be somewhat tarnished characters, if even it chances that both of them desert their post, the commune will be able to make shift by itself, and will not be half so troubled as if the bread had suddenly risen a sixth of its price. What makes the bulk of the population care much about the State is not so much the services received from it, as the contributions exacted by it. In despotic states, which interest us particularly in this study, the conception of the maintenance of order is somewhat strange, as everybody knows. Here the Government, though exerting itself to prevent people cutting each other's throats, and stealing each other's property (this being the privilege of officials) is still more anxious to prevent people from questioning and criticising its own problematic wisdom, and honesty, and justice. Here preservation of order means dead silence in respect of people's wrong, passive obedience to all the exactions of the governing caste, obstructing and stifling of any useful work which private individuals should be disposed to do for the community. Such states present a small but well-organised body of people, who, having command over the military and civil forces of the community,—the army and the police,—enforce their will on the masses of unorganised nation.

Now, if we suppose that, notwithstanding the obstruction, the country is happy enough to bring forward a body of men sufficiently strong to overpower and overthrow this organised oppression, it would be unnecessary, unwise, even cowardly and criminal toward the community and posterity if these men should postpone their attack a day longer. To the honour of humanity it must be said that this was never the case. The generous love for freedom, and pity for the oppressed country, always urged people to the struggle rather before there was sufficient strength to carry on the combat. And in all countries the way to freedom has been bedewed with the blood of martyrs. Even the great French revolution of 1789-93—the most momentous popular rising known in modern history—was begun by a handful of men, and carried out by the small minority of the population among the sympathising, consenting, or indifferent masses. This is a fact peremptorily proved by all the investigators of this epoch, its detractors and admirers included, from Ziebel and Taine down to modern revolutionists of the reddest dye. And there was certainly no revolution which commanded such considerable numerical strength as this great one. The other continental revolutions, made under the influence of this great one, were numerically far less strong. If some tyrannical government had been overthrown by a mere handful of men, one could only say, so much the better. The violence of revolutionary proceeding has, of course, its drawback: it always produces a temporary disorder in the sphere into which it is carried. But as this disorder is localised within the narrow political domain, it affects really only the surface of national life; the more so that only such deep and long revolutions as that of 1789-93 in France affect to a certain degree the inferior branches of administration—those concerned with the every-day work for the maintenance of order and security. Generally they begin and finish in the high or central spheres of government. If, nevertheless, they are so heavily felt by the nations, it is only because, and as far as, they affect indirectly or incidentally the economical province.

Thus the two revolutions — the political and economical — differ considerably by the mode of their realisation. The element of violence, which is inefficient, almost inapplicable for the latter, plays a very essential and important part in the former. The political regeneration of a nation, the infusion of liberty into the habits, customs, social and political intercourse, cannot be done by a sudden stroke. What was created by time requires time to be undone. But the starting-point for such a work was always a sudden and violent outburst of national indignation and enthusiasm, bearing the glorious name of revolution.

III.

In the natural course of things the acquisition of political freedom must precede any serious attempt at social reorganisation. It is self-evident. For how to set to work without having first freed the workers' hands from bondage? Had all the countries, at least in Europe, advanced at the same pace on the way of their internal development, no great complication in their march to progress could have arisen. All would become politically free, and then, secure from all obstruction, proceed in the way of social reorganisation. But it is not so. Owing to the difference of the natural condition of the countries, their geographical position and historical peculiarities, the European states of to-day, though all unmistakably progressing in their culture, have distanced each other no less than for almost three centuries, or something like, in their political conditions. Whilst England has almost forgotten the epochs of its violent civil struggle for political freedom, which are looming in the darkness, confounded with recollections of the Middle Ages, Russia remains under an autocracy much more absolute than that of Henry VIII.

The bulk of continental Europe has awakened to liberty only since 1848, and in France herself, which has given the signal for and led them, the first victory of freedom was followed by its defeat, which necessitated several new revolutions. What could be more natural than the idea of applying the quick medicine of popular insurrection, which proved so successful against political oppression, to the healing of economical wrongs? Thus arose the idea of the "social revolution" as such.

Such theories were particularly popular among the socialists of the Latin race, owing partly to their more impatient temper, but still more to the fact that the political revolutions have played a much more important part in their immediate past than in Germany. But even in these countries the practical life enforced by-and-by a more rational conception of the social revolution. It is impossible to provoke an artificial revolution, and some few attempts in this direction in Italy made a complete fiasco. The working men organisations, stepping into the field both in France and Italy, put the social question from the domain of revolutionary metaphysics on to practical ground. The fraction which proclaimed violent insurrections as the only means for realising socialism was reduced to almost imperceptible dimensions.

When in the year 1882 it became suddenly most conspicuous, most spoken of, becoming unexpectedly the bugbear of the peace-and-ease-loving *bourgeoisie*, a new method was invented by which every single individual, with little or no assistance at all, shall wage war against the existing *régime:* I mean the introduction of dynamite as a political agent. Dynamite outrages began in France in this year, and very soon found imitators.

What could produce this strange fit of dynamite epidemic?

I think we shall be very near the truth in admitting that the chief factor in determining this outbreak was the example of Russian Nihilists: a case not devoid of interest for a student of social psychology.

In all times there were violent attempts against various representatives of the governments—kings and their ministers. Very often such attempts were followed by a series of three or four outrages, committed in different countries, but closely following each other; then subsiding for a long number of years until a new stroke roused the seemingly sleeping destructive spirit, and a new file-firing began. This suggestive fact can only be explained by the tendency for imitation, which is observable in mankind.

One very interesting example of the contagious influence of such acts is presented by the five attempts against the crowned heads which took place at short intervals from May 1878 to December 1879, and then dropped off, and have never been repeated since. What could be the cause of this sudden file-firing? What the scope of attempting against a constitutional sovereign who, *de jure* and *de facto*, cannot be answerable for anything which is done in the state? But the thing will become quite clear if we admit the possibility of moral contagion in certain acts which strike the imagination. All these attempts followed immediately the attempt of Vèra Zassoulitch, who shot General Trepoff, the Russian police officer, who ordered the flogging of a political prisoner for having omitted to take off his hat to him. There was, of course, the widest difference between these acts. But this might mean something in the case of a rational tendency, but nothing at all in the case of an epidemic contagion. Zassulitch's shot, and still more her acquittal by the jury, found the most tremendous reverberation throughout all the civilised world, creating thus the exciting atmosphere in which the Russian idea of avenging public wrongs by attempts against representatives of power could assume any shape, or receive any practical application, according to the circumstances and individual peculiarity. And the brief but violent regicidal epidemic arose. No single act of Russian terrorists has agitated so strongly European public opinion as the Zassulitch affair. But what they failed to do separately they did, and more effectively combined. When, after the first attempts against functionaries, the Nihilists began their dynamite duel with the autocrat in person, they acquired the most tremendous popularity throughout the whole world. The mystery, the fascinating courage and spirit of self-sacrifice, and the wild energy of the gigantic struggle, were particularly apt to strike the imagination. The partisans of order and legality, at any price and under any circumstances, objected to the means. But even they were dazzled by the Nihilists, who for years were the living romance of the whole European press. As to the extreme parties, both political and social, we are proud and thankful to say that from the very beginning they were with us. Radicals and socialists—among whom the majority were by no means partisans of violence—were willing to consider the deep wrongs of the Russian people, and warm in their sympathies; they sided with us, and did us that justice which other parties are beginning to do now. Among them the Nihilist struggle won from the beginning an unconditional approbation. It was the same with the great mass of working men of all countries and of all shades of opinion. Having no vested interests to defend, they were less exacting in their judgment. The longer the struggle lasted, the greater was the interest in it and the enthusiasm for it. And it was quite natural that in some individuals the example might have proved contagious. And so it did. The European dynamite period was of an epidemical, and not of a sporadic kind. It is only fair to add that a very perspicacious writer, whom I have had already opportunity to mention—Professor Michel Dragomanoff—had forewarned Europe that such a fact *must* happen almost two years before it really happened. In his pamphlet, "Tyrannicide en Russie et l'Action de l'Europe Occidentale," Geneva, 1881, after having shown that the terrorists are struggling for political freedom, and the present Russian crisis is a political one similar to that which England underwent in the sixteenth century, he concludes: "But this Russian crisis, however different by its character from the socialist movement of Western Europe, cannot be carried on without influencing to a certain degree the latter. It will impart to it its bloody character, exciting those passionate rather than rational instincts which are latent among the disinherited classes, even in the most advanced countries. This is the point on which every political man in Europe must reflect, and this is also the reason for the intervention of Europe in the Russian crisis" (pp. 12-13). This prognostication proved to be true. And is not the fact of the subsiding of dynamite attempts in Europe due to a very considerable extent to the absence of the exciting influence from Russia?

But will it always be so? Certainly not. The Russian struggle for liberty practically began only some ten years ago. With the quick intellectual growth of Russians, and the rashness of all our social process, the crisis cannot be protracted very long. It began with greater intensity than in other European countries, and must end sooner. But it would be pusillanimous for us to hope and presume to sweep away the autocracy with a few pounds of dynamite. Our hardest strife is in the future; and in this strife all arms must and will be employed to atone for the enormous disparity of material strength. This cannot be helped; and this spectacle cannot be lost upon Europe. Thus it is not the success of the Russian revolution, but the protraction of the sanguinary struggle, that really threatens the tranquillity of European people. This would be a sad eventuality of course. We have every reason to desire that the great social reconstruction in which all the advanced countries are concerned should be carried out as orderly as possible. Because what will be the best of good fortune for Europe will be the best of examples for Russia. But every country's first duty is towards itself. The historical mission of our generation is to overthrow the ferocious Asiatic despotism which is stifling our country to death. And we will overthrow it by whatever means we find within our reach. The civilised Europeans have as little right to urge us to desist from our violences as a man who hears groans coming from next door, where some diabolic torture is inflicted on a human being, has to say to the victim, "Keep silent, because your groans prevent me from digesting comfortably my good dinner." It is in a more generous way that the thinking men of free countries should intervene in the fierce strife raging on the eastern plain. They cannot prevent it. But they will undoubtedly shorten it and minimise its violence by affording the cause of Russian liberty the assistance which can reasonably be afforded, and which Russian people have the right to expect from the public opinion of the more advanced nations.

VI.

A REVOLT OR A REVOLUTION?

A REVOLT OR A REVOLUTION?

(*Conclusion.*)

I.

It is a well-established truth that foreigners, provided they are sufficiently well informed, are often the best judges of a country. They possess, in the first place, the most valuable requisite for dispassionate observation, that thorough impartiality which it is difficult for a native to attain. Besides, as they are new to the country, their senses and intellect are more keenly alive to peculiarities that pass unnoticed by those born and educated in it. At the time of some great crisis in the history of a nation it is often given to foreigners to discover the first symptoms of coming events. When at the end of the last century French society was indulging in humanitarian dreams, it was an Englishman, Arthur Young, who predicted the approach of the great revolution.

Russia had not the good fortune to attract so much attention from European nations as France under Louis XVI. The Russian crisis was revealed to Europe by the echo of dynamite explosions, and not announced in anticipation by some far-seeing traveller. Before the Nihilist struggle began there was hardly a man in Europe who cared about Russian liberty, and the conspiracies of which now and then the European press was informed were regarded as mere childish enterprises, having no serious meaning and no future. Since then the times have considerably changed. The partisans of the Russian Government might cry themselves hoarse, repeating that the Nihilists were maniacs, fond of destruction for destruction's sake. All sensible and thinking men felt that there must be something wrong in Russia if hundreds and thousands of people, showing after all no symptom of madness, sacrifice their future, their prosperity, and often their lives for getting something better. Attention once awakened, the truth could not fail to be discovered. There is no divergence of opinion any more among all serious and conscientious investigators of Russian life as to the seriousness and depth of the Russian crisis.

I will quote only one of them, undoubtedly the best and most universally recognised authority on the matter,—M. Leroy Beaulieu. His name is sufficiently well known in England to render comment unnecessary. Here are some extracts of the conclusion of his two volumes, " L'Empire des Tzars et les Russes' (vol. ii., pp. 605, 608, 611-15).

"To sum up, Russia, according to our opinion, is compelled to begin, and that very soon, the practice of modern free institutions. By what door will she enter? It is beyond our power to predict the course of events, or to point out to her the path to be followed. On the part of a foreigner this would be presumption. What we know as quite certain is, that it is high time for her to start on this journey.

"For a long time the most advanced among Russians were little inclined to hasten with their wishes the hour when the nation should be put in possession of political rights. Some months before the last Bulgarian campaign an intelligent and liberal Russian, discussing the subject, said to me, 'The constitution will be for the next reign. It is better for Russia to have it fifteen years later than fifteen years too early.' These words seemed the embodiment of wisdom, and I confess to having admired their prudence myself, whilst acknowledging this truth. Are we as certain of the accuracy of this sentence now? After-events have induced me to doubt it. The disorderly agitation of the young generation, the nervous irritability of society, which increases constantly; the evident impossibility of preserving the *status quo*, and the difficulty of breaking it up under pressure of threats from the revolutionists,—all this forces us to ask ourselves, if it would not be better not to wait until the hour of political reform rings out, but to grant the needed reforms at once.

"The excitements and disappointments of the Bulgarian war; the implacable campaign of the terrorists; the confusion of a Government obliged to try uselessly, one after another, all its ministers and advisers,—all this has in a few years strikingly ripened the question, if not the nation. The whole of the educated classes seem to have arrived at such a state of mind that to beguile their appetite for political reforms and freedom, the Imperial Government will have no other expedient than external diversions, heroical adventures.

"For these Russia is not prepared either as to diplomacy, finance, or the army. Like our ephemeral French empires this Government, after ten centuries of duration, will be more and more forced to choose between internal reforms and external wars, between liberty and glory. In default of one it will be obliged to give the other. This dilemma, well known in France, will impose itself more and more on Russia. And the last Oriental campaign has shown her how hazardous and uncertain is this game, even in the case of victory. There is, indeed, a kind of vicious circle. Often war lays open the sores of a country, makes palpable the vices of the Government, and the necessity of control by the people.

"That is precisely what has been done at an interval of twenty years by the two Oriental wars. The invasion of the Crimea was the starting-point of the emancipation of the serfs and the great laws of Alexander II. The double campaign of Bulgaria, followed by no general reform, not having been the signal for political emancipation, became the starting-point of revolutionary terrorism and of the Tzaricide."

I would say a few words on the subject of the influence of the Bulgarian war in connection with the opinion, quoted by M. Leroy Beaulieu, of a wise Russian statesman on the usefulness of postponing political reforms. There is a considerable difference in the effect of the two Oriental wars. The reign of Nicholas I. was one of pure *mili-*

tarism, a feeble example of which is to be observed in modern Prussia. The Crimean defeat was a condemnation of the whole system of Nicholas I., and had, therefore, the same moral effect as a defeat of the modern German Empire in some external war would have to-day. The reign of Alexander II. was that of internal reforms, initiated at the beginning of his reign. The defeat of *his* system consisted in the abortion of all his reforms, which began to be strongly felt ten years before the Bulgarian war. The political crisis which the general disappointment gradually brought about arrived at its acutest point before the Oriental war broke out. Our whole literature was full of it. The Bulgarian campaign had certainly its share in embittering the crisis, but this influence was a secondary one, not at all comparable with that of the Crimean war. It is quite certain that, had there been no Bulgarian war at all, the Nihilist struggle would have begun all the same. The elements for it were quite ready in the general disposition and spirit of Russian society, and in those of the secret organisations of revolutionists. And yet, just at this period, M. Leroy Beaulieu's wiseacre indulged in idle talk about political reforms as premature, and the utility of their being postponed for some fifteen years! Is this not a proof that even for certain classes of Russians something stronger than the outcry of "penny-a-liners" was necessary to bring them to think and observe what was going on in the country under their feet?

" To the struggle with a foreigner succeeded an

internal war of much greater length, greater ferocity; and, notwithstanding the small number of soldiers who entered the lists, of more expense to the country and the Government. This war with an invisible and always re-appearing Alexander III. cannot end by a treaty of peace as his father did with the war in 1855. It is the soul of the young generation that he must pacify. This he cannot do otherwise than by reconciling his government with the spirit of the century, without being influenced by the threats of some, and the flatteries of others, without being diverted by the pride, the fear, or the presumption of false security.

" From whatever point of view we consider it, a liberal revolution seems to us the best, or rather the only possible solution of the crisis. Seek as long as we like, we shall discover no other. Does it mean, then, that all will be settled by its introduction? Certainly not. The supplanting of the present *régime* by another will be not so much a solution as a new starting-point, a beginning rather than an end. Liberty and political constitutions are like marriage, which in novels and plays appears often as a solution, but in reality is only the inauguration of a new life with its toil, its struggle, and its trials. In entering upon the way to which public opinion is prompting it, Russia will certainly have her difficulties, her troubles, and even her perils if you like. But these will be the troubles and perils common to all modern governments. Such a change alone will be of good to her. Her struggles, errors, and even her disappointments will become useful to her. With the *status quo*, on the contrary, there is nothing to gain. There are dangers which must be hurried on, were it only in order not to increase them. There are cases when the safest of expedients is that which is the boldest, when there is more to risk in risking nothing. Such is the position of the heir of Alexander II.

"How many times have the French asked themselves at what precise moment the Revolution could have been arrested as it sank towards anarchy and terror? Nobody could point out this moment with certainty. To us it seems that this moment was already lost at the epoch of the convocation of the *États Généraux*. The only means to prevent the revolution was to outstrip it. The Russia of Alexander III., though differing singularly from the France of Louis XVI., is, I think, precisely in the same position. The surest means to impede the revolution is to outstrip it by giving its initiation to the Government. 'Reforms from above, or revolutions from below,' said Alexander II. at the beginning of his reign,

"There are, however, changes so momentous to be made, that we ask ourselves anxiously whether they can be effected peacefully without trouble or revolution. So was it in France at the downfall of the feudal *régime*. Will it be otherwise in Russia with her political transformation? It will depend perhaps upon the ability and good fortune of the dynasty. Nations and societies have what we may call their moulting time: great transformations that can hardly be effected without disturbance and suffering, without a sort of external decay or apparent death. But let not appearances deceive us;

if Russia has to pass through similar trials, and issue temporarily enfeebled, this will be for her, as for France of 1789, a crisis of growth, and not the convulsion of agony and decrepitude.

"And if in Russia at the end of the nineteenth century, as in France at the end of the eighteenth, a revolution becomes unavoidable, what will be the result of it for Russia and Europe? What new order of things will issue from this chaos?

"In many respects a Russian revolution (if it be anything else than a disordered and brief interregnum) will have a stamp of originality and novelty which are not to be found in any revolution of other European nations. The West had already its revolution in the French, since all the nations of Germano-Latin origin have more or less felt its influence, borrowed its doctrines, tasted its benefits and its evils. Our revolution was, so to say, the redemption of feudal Europe. But it may be said that patriarchal Eastern Europe, the Slavonic world, awaits still its revolution, or what must represent it. And whence, if not from Russia, can the initiative of it come? Viewed in this light, a Russian revolution might be the greatest of historical events since the French revolution, to which, at an interval of one century, it would be the natural supplement.

"The presumptuous hope of creating a new type of society, which the reactionary Slavophiles claim for their country, is repeated in a different form, but with the same assurance, by many Russian revolutionists. They dream that the Russian revolution will completely outdo our revolutions, which were all individualistic, profitable to the *bourgeoisie* rather than to the masses of the people, whilst the Russian revolution will bring into the world a new really popular gospel, having more of a socialistic stamp than a political one, adapted to the wants of the Slavonic people, and presenting at the same time to the West an example worthy of imitation.

"And really a Russian revolution, which must almost certainly arrive at a kind of agrarian socialism, cannot help being different from what we have seen elsewhere. It is precisely in a revolution that Russia will have the greatest facility of showing herself original, and of producing something new and purely Slavonic. But at what price ? with what losses for civilisation and science ?

"Priority in revolutions is, moreover, a kind of *primato* too dearly bought, too perilous for us to hope for on behalf of Russia. Much better will it be for her not to have such fallacious ambitions, to march by more modest and by safer ways. And this all the more, as in such cases the time seemingly gained to-day is often lost to-morrow, and the way which was thought the shortest is found to be the longest. . . . ."

I have translated these pages inspired by true humanity and sincere goodwill to our unhappy country and its freedom. For them every Russian whom they will reach will be deeply thankful to the author. And certainly I could not find a more solid basis for some further considerations than this summing up of many years' study and observations on the part of a scholar whose impartiality as well as competency cannot be questioned.

Thus, M. Leroy Beaulieu entertains no doubt as

to the imminence of a Russian catastrophe, or as to its sweeping character. He thinks that the momentous crisis cannot be arrested or prevented; but it may be either sanguinary or pacific, according to the line of conduct of the government as to the introduction of political freedom into Russia at short notice or too late. The possible peacefulness of the solution of the Russian crisis, according to M. Leroy Beaulieu, is, however, only comparative. He greatly doubts whether so great a transformation as he foresees, even initiated by the existing government, can avoid the reef of popular disturbances, and he does his best to prepare his readers to accept the unavoidable, and tries to minimise, as far as possible, the importance of the temporary disturbances that must be.

II.

Without absolutely denying the possibility of some temporary and local disorders, we think that the above-mentioned apprehensions are based rather on abstract historical analogies than on the realities of Russian life. It is quite certain that the inauguration of political freedom in Russia—whatever be the door by which it enters—will be the starting-point of a series of agrarian and social reforms, much more radical than those which accompanied the French revolution. This is the reason why that very modest thing called the "Constitution" is worth having and struggling for, not solely for its own sake, but also for the sake of the masses of our people. But if we throw off preconceived historical notions, and look at the present condition of Russia, we shall see that at the present moment at least there are really no elements to justify such apprehensions. That which distinguishes Russia from France at the end of the eighteenth century as well as from all modern European States is its great uniformity. It is a peasant's state in the fullest possible acceptation of the phrase. Official statistics show a rural class constituting about 82 per cent. of the whole number of inhabitants. This is three times more than in France, and five times more than in Great Britain. But in reality, as every Russian knows, the proportion of the rural class is still greater. The people inscribed in the official registers of population as "citizens," or inhabitants of towns, also belong to a considerable extent to the rural class. The small provincial towns with less than ten thousand inhabitants are in reality great villages, the bulk of whose population is devoted to agriculture. Even in the larger towns a considerable number of the inhabitants of the suburbs are mere peasants.

The peasants are certainly the most powerful class of the Russian nation, I may say the only class in the scientific acceptation of the word. They present, moreover, a remarkable uniformity in their economical aspirations, political organisation, and traditional code of laws.

The class which by its social importance is next to that of the peasants is certainly the educated class, representing the spiritual forces of the nation, —its brains and nerves,—as the peasants represent its bones and muscles. This class, however, as the reader may remember, embodies no special interests distinct from those of the peasants. They can hardly be called a privileged class at all, for they depend on the work of their brain, as the workmen on that of their hands. Their material prosperity, as well as social influence and position, depends entirely on that of the peasants. If the peasants prosper, the educated classes will prosper also; if the peasants become masters of their destiny, enjoy freedom, and real and not fictitious self-government, the educated men will acquire all the political and social influence due to their capacity as managers, teachers, political representatives of the masses. They can have no other function. And we have seen that by their education, their former history, and the traditions of three generations, our intellectual classes, far from recoiling from—are most willing to accept—this mission of devoting their forces to the service of the masses, the most glorious office for people possessing the benefits of high education.

When the free political institution replaces the present bureaucratic despotism—the third great force, —that of the state, which is now striving by hook or by crook to prevent the union and mutual understanding of the two above-mentioned elements, will be placed in their hands. It might, it will require a certain time of political training and education to enable the peasants to use to their advantage the representative institutions they will receive. It is very likely that at first many of them will consider the sending of deputies to a Zemsky Sobor (a Parliament) as a new burden, of which they must get rid as cheaply as possible. But *is* this the possible source of "disturbances," "troubles," "convulsions," and the like?

And when this transitory period passes, and the wishes of the masses are represented effectively and not nominally, where is the force in Russia capable of resisting their fulfilment? In France there was a powerful clergy and a feudal nobility that in some provinces preserved its traditional influence. Do we see something like this in modern Russia? Our clergy never had any political influence at all, and now it has morally ruined itself by accepting the vile part of spy and police agent, assigned to it by the dying autocracy. As to aristocracy, Russia has nothing of the kind. Our slave-owning nobility can claim this name with as little right as the planters of Virginia amongst their liberated negro slaves. In our day there is, I may say, no nobility. Only the great men, who are at the same time members of the high bureaucracy, can supply their losses as landowners by direct subsidies from the State, and thus withstand the general depression. The bulk of our landed gentry is totally ruined, and its land culture is in such a miserable condition that their class would be not at all displeased to give up the land for a very moderate compensation from the State. Such is at least the statement of those among these classes from whom I could obtain information. The only class—or better, the only set of people—interested in the maintenance of the present ruinous and absurd land system are the new land forestallers, the *miroieds*,—eaters of the *mir*, as the peasants call them. Profiting by the dependent and utterly downtrodden condition of the peasants, these professional usurers have engrossed a good deal of communal land, and ensnared the peasants, reducing them into a state of economical slavery, very similar to the old one. It is not this gang of robbers, universally hated by the peasants and despised by the educated classes, that will be able to incite disturbances.

No, in Russia no reform tending to the real benefit of the agricultural masses has to apprehend anything worth the name of troubles. The uniformity of the Russian nation, which was the source of our unhappy political *régime*, has at least a compensation in the facility and simplicity of our future social reforms

As to the towns—where once the concession of political freedom satisfies the aspiration of the whole of the educated class, and opens to it the best prospect for the future—the impossibility of any insurrectional attempt is too evident to need any explanation.

In giving to the government of Alexander that most thoughtful suggestion, that the concession of political freedom would be profitable even to the dynasty, the French scholar might have dispensed with mentioning, as a drawback, the quite theoretical danger of threatening disturbances. For nothing worthy this name is really to be expected in such cases.

And yet it is the most fallacious of all hopes to expect that the liberal evolution will be initiated by the Tzar's spontaneous impulse. The implicit confidence in the possibility of such an event is the only point in which the opinion of Mr. Leroy Beaulieu will be contradicted by every Russian who has followed rationally modern Russian history. There is nothing to expect from the government of Alexander III. I doubt whether there are two opinions on the matter in Russia, and at present, after five years of experience, it is hardly necessary to discuss the point with Europeans. It is also a mistake to think that it was the Nihilists' attempts that frightened the Government out of its poor wits, preventing it from doing something rational, as Mr. Leroy Beaulieu and many Europeans with him are inclined to think. The reactionary policy of Alexander II., in all the last fifteen years of the twenty-five of his reign, was the cause and not the result of the Nihilistic insurrection. As to the third Alexander, we have only to appeal to the memory of our contemporaries to establish the fact that his internal policy becomes more reactionary in proportion as the catastrophe of the 13th March recedes in the background. Having begun by maintaining Count Loris Melikoff, he passed to Count Ignatieff with his jokes of representative commissions, and ended by Count Tolstoi's ministry, which is obscurantism and reaction with no hope or remorse. If the Government has made such a use of the five years' respite, given to it by the revolution, what indeed is to be hoped from the good graces of the Gatchina court? The dense net, woven of selfishness, conceit, cowardice, of dark, impenetrable ignorance prevailing in high circles, can be broken only by the effect of external forces, coming from the world outside it.

I am most willing to admit that these external forces are not exclusively material ones. There is no way open to the manifestation of public opinion in Russia, as freedom of the press and of speech are entirely suppressed. Even the right of petition ing, so humble that it can hardly be called a right, is considered a " political crime," if exercised without special permission of the administration. An "arbitrary petition," even drawn up in the most respectful and humble terms, if referring to something like political freedom, is punishable with imprisonment, exile to Siberia, or elsewhere, as many examples prove. In such a country the only way to give vent to the opinions and wishes of the nation is by what may be called with the awkward term of "peaceful rebellion."

A manifestation, made in disregard of police proscription and prohibitions by a large body of people, will make it impossible for the Government to punish the delinquents, which at first the Government certainly will do. Such a manifestation, if made boldly and frankly, might have the greatest moral effect both in Russia and in Europe. It is highly desirable, and it would be most opportune at any time. It would be childish to expect that with the absurd Government we have the misfortune to possess, any amount of moral pressure alone will be sufficient to induce it to lay down its arms. Russia has already shown an instructive example of a very general manifestation of public opinion in favour of political liberty. It was in 1860, in the epoch of the emancipation of the serfs. But this movement failed to produce any effect, because in this epoch of general confidence in the good faith of the Government it could not be supported by more impressive actions on the part of Russian patriots. On the other hand, the great terrorist struggle with the Tzardom was within a hair's breadth of forcing the autocracy to listen to reason. Ample proof of this can be found even in M. Leroy Beaulieu's writings (especially in *Revue des Deux Mondes* for October, 1881), which show that the terrorists were not so foolish after all as some people are inclined to believe, and the theory about violence producing only a recrudescence of reaction is not quite an unimpeachable one. They did not give freedom to their country; hundreds of noble heroes and martyrs perished in the unequal struggle without realising their generous dream, because they were left almost alone in the field. They received no support worth the name either from the bulk of Russian progressive parties or from European public opinion, because the extreme rashness of our revolutionary movement prevented them from being known and accepted for what they really were. And the reports circulated by the police about the Nihilists' destructive anarchical tendencies and complete absence of any positive ideals frightened the good people in Russia and in Europe. Thus the great movement for liberty of 1878-82 proved to be as one-sided as that of 1859-62. The former was supported by forcible pressure only, as the latter only by moral. The amalgamation of all parties in Russia, and the growing disposition of the public opinion of the civilised world to do justice to the champions of Russian freedom, are a guarantee that this fatal dualism will not be repeated any more. The physical attack to be efficient must be supported by the moral action of the public opinion of the country and of the world. The moral action, in order to become effective, must be supported by force of arms, by the effective or imminent insurrection, which we have analysed in this book, showing its scope, its methods, and the forces which are at its command. This is in reality not a *revolution*, but only a *revolt*. Because by revolution a universal catastrophe is generally meant. The insurrection we are speaking of cannot be of this nature. From the brief analysis of it we have made in our first chapters, the reader might infer that the elements on which until now the insurrection can depend are town's people. There is no danger that such an insurrection could be turned to the exclusive advantage of the people living in the towns, thus necessitating perhaps a new insurrection in favour of the peasants, as a very thoughtful English critic has observed.* Democracy is *imposed* in a country like Russia. Whatever the elements which a town insurrection places at the head of the affair, they will be obliged to make at once the greatest agrarian concessions in favour of the peasants as the only means to interest them in the maintenance of the new *régime*, and prevent their being made an instrument of a counter-revolution. On the other hand, it is as improbable that an insurrection, similar to that of the Decembrists of 1825, would be a signal for a general rising of the agricultural masses, since there are no elements as yet in our villages to echo it. The rising in the capital may certainly have such an effect; but later on, not now. At present a successful insurrection in the towns, a revolt made by the common efforts of those to whom the present *régime* is no longer tolerable, will

* *Bradford Observer*, September 4th, 1885.

prevent and render unnecessary the destructive, tremendous, and chaotic revolution of the masses, prognosticated by Mr. Leroy Beaulieu as approaching and imminent.

Thus into his alternative: either a voluntary resignation at short notice of the autocracy—which is impossible,—or a revolution. I beg to introduce a modification: the alternative is—either a revolt or a revolution.

III.

Which of the two shall we have? It is difficult to give an answer which would be taken as an impartial one, free from the suggestions of party spirit and party hope, and not open to the accusation of party optimism. Let us rather try to understand the working and the mutual relation of the elements which are working together towards the revolt or the revolution.

What is, to begin with, the immediate, the fundamental, the most palpable cause of the instability of the autocracy in Russia? It is its own insufficiency and inadequacy to the task incumbent upon it. Protected by force of bayonets it can withstand as yet the universal desire of the whole of educated Russia and the attacks of the few. But nothing can prevent the system from having its natural effects, the first of which is the gradual impoverishment of the agricultural masses. The frightful misery of the bulk of our peasantry, which the official press decried as the invention of the socialist dreamers in 1873, is now a fact admitting no discussion, acknowledged even by the official commission of "experts," and amply proved by official statistics. I will mention briefly only a few concluding facts from indisputable authorities. Professor Janson, in his "Essay on the Peasant's Allotment," has shown the deterioration of peasant's agriculture, the insufficiency of land, the insufficiency of pasture, the diminution in the number of cattle, insufficiency of bread. Mr. One, one of our best authorities on economical questions, has made the stirring discovery that the average consumption of bread, which is almost the exclusive food of our peasantry, has diminished during the years 1861-79 at about 14 per cent. (*Slovo* for 1878, p. 120). To conclude: quite recently—the 18th December, 1885—a report on the sanitary condition of Russia was read at the regular meeting of the Society of Russian Surgeons, the well-known Mr. S. P. Botkin, body-surgeon to the Emperor, in the chair. This report points out the enormous mortality among Russian people, surpassing normally what in other countries is considered the precursor of epidemic disease. In England, when the death-rate approaches 23 in 1,000, a regular inquiry and sanitation of the district is prescribed by law, the case being recognised as an abnormal one In Russia the death-rate per 1,000 was above 31, sometimes as high as 35. And the first cause of this frightful mortality is stated simply and eloquently to be *deficiency of food (bread)*. *Novosty*, 17th (30th), December, 1885.

Neither is the chief cause of this wretched misery— I may say, this chronic starvation—a secret. It lies in the enormously high taxation, on the one hand,

and the no less enormous malversation of the inferior agents of the administration, to whom our peasants are subjected, on the other.

In all states enjoying political freedom the taxes are distributed in a certain proportion to the wealth of the citizens, so that the rich classes bear a very considerable part of the state expenses. But in despotic states it is the opposite line which is always followed. Here the superior classes have almost complete immunity from taxation, which lies almost entirely on the poor classes alone. There is not a single exception to this rule, and indeed there can hardly be any. Free, self-governing countries alone can lay heavy taxes on the superior classes, without recoiling before the unavoidable consequences of this. The despotic must be content with ignorant peasants, accustomed to consider taxes as a calamity inherent to earthly existence, and paying taxes, however heavy, without inquiring what is done with them. The educated classes, when giving up their money, will jealously observe how it is managed; their hearts will bleed at the spectacle of its dissipation. And the outcry for the right of managing it by means of national representation will become more clamorous, and certainly more general than at the sight of the most cynical violation of individual liberties. I have already mentioned how prudently the Russian Government has behaved in this matter, when in 1871 the representatives of our privileged classes, all the thirty-four Russian zemstvos, were in favour of the freeing of the peasant from exorbitant taxes, and petitioned for the introduction of a progressive income tax on all citizens.

The Tzar, "father of the peasants," cut short these democratic desires. And from his point of view he acted very wisely, unwilling as he was to add a new and powerful stimulus to rebellion to the many already existing.

Thus the famishing Russian peasants are the chief, not to say the sole tax-payers, as they have been before, and will be in the future, as long as the autocracy exists. Of the total budget of the State, the peasants, possessing only 30 per cent. of the cultivable soil, pay no less than 83 per cent., leaving to landowners and capitalists, having twice as much landed property and five times as much capital, only 17 per cent. (According to Prince Variltchekoff's estimation the share of the peasants is 90 per cent., and that of the other classes only 10 per cent.) Such a burden must inevitably crush under its weight the peasants whom the emancipation of 1861—of the greatest moral benefit—left very badly off as far as concerns their material conditions. Our *moujik* is no longer a citizen paying his share of contribution to the State expenses. He is virtually a serf of the State, obliged to give it in taxes about one half, sometimes more, of his whole work time,* —in the whole, *more* than they gave to their *seigneurs* in the times of serfdom. And when times are bad, and no extra revenue is forthcoming, economy is made as to nourishment at the expense of health and life, as we have just seen. For the

* I mean all the work done by a peasant during the year, both on the land and in the towns. As to the land, which is the base of taxation, it is often taxed *beyond* its total net produce. See Professor Janson.

State is a hard master, exacting unpaid taxes with a cruelty which no modern conqueror would apply in extorting contributions from a conquered land. The insolvent are pitilessly flogged, and when this punishment produces no effect, all the property of the peasant—cattle, tools, houses—is sold by auction. And yet, notwithstanding the panic dread inspired by such summary punishment, every year there are millions of arrears in the peasant payments, and every year whole villages, sometimes whole districts, are invaded by bands of soldiers and policemen, conducting the auctioneer, followed by a motley crew of merchants, and the work of destruction begins, leaving the village or the district devastated as by a conflagration, and the whole population reduced to irremediable ruin.

I hardly need dwell on the second cause of the ruin of the peasants, the malversations of the inferior police agents, administrators, those anxious to be elected headmen, communal clerks, and all who are willing to rob them with the easily obtainable assistance of the administration. I will only say that the amount of plundering and material harm (without speaking of the other aspects) produced in this way is simply enormous. The malversation going on in the superior spheres of imperial administration is great, but the wrong done to the totally helpless and ignorant peasants entirely eclipses this. And the autocracy is as impotent to prevent these malversations as to disburden the peasants of their weight of taxes. If changing the system of distribution of taxes means national representation at short notice, the only remedy for these abuses is a free press, the free access of educated and really "well-intentioned" elements to villages. This, in the eyes of the Government at least, is social revolution at once.

Thus the process of the progressive impoverishment of the agricultural masses goes on, and must go on its way, irremediable, fatal. And as certainly it brings in a country like Russia the total economical, financial, and political decomposition of the State, with all its natural consequences.

IV.

This process of undermining the very foundation of the State is accompanied by another process of quite an opposite character; the continual and very rapid growth of the culture, industry, and enlightenment concentrated in the towns. The despotic *régime* exercises its baleful influence everywhere and in everything, in towns as well as in villages. But the townspeople are much cleverer than the peasants; they have thousands of ways of escaping the heavy hand of the Government; they possess the greater force which numbers give, and the Government shows them always a certain regard. Thus the action of the existing *régime* on town life is only debilitating.

I have already spoken of the wonderful progress of manufacturing industry. Whilst agriculture is in continual depression, and, notwithstanding the extension of great culture, the average value of agricultural produce remains stationary, being about 1,800 million roubles yearly, the value of manufacturing industry is continually increasing. From 1865 to 1878 its value increased to about five times, and since then has increased again twice as much.

The population of the towns is rapidly increasing. In 1861 there were only six towns having more than 100,000 inhabitants; now the number is thirteen, more than double. The number of provincial towns having more than 10,000 inhabitants increased in the same period from 185 to 315. And the total town population has augmented about thirty-three per cent.

The greatest progress was, however, made in the domain of education, which is all the more striking, as society had to overcome on this point relentless obstruction on the part of the Government. The best results were obtained, of course, in the higher branches of education. Thus, in the last ten years alone, the number of pupils in the colleges has increased from 30,000 to 66,000; and the number of students in the universities from 6,200 to 10,400. And all those who know anything about Russia are aware that the Government did all it could to tamper with the high schools, considered to be the nurseries of revolutionary agitation. Were it not for these artificial obstacles the progress would have been three times as great as it is. But even the progress achieved is wonderful, and hardly equalled in another European country. Nothing, indeed, could give better proof of the vigorous vitality of the young Russian nation, or be of better promise for its future.

The popular classes of the towns are not excluded from the benefits of better education, and, let us observe, show no less anxiety about it. In the capital, for example, the progress made in this branch is one of the best trophies of our embryonic self-government; from 1872 to 1882 the number of schools has increased from 13 to 158, and the number of pupils from some few scores which the old schools hardly taught at all to 6,000 well-taught children, the majority of whom belong to the working class.

A century ago the culture introduced under the auspices of Peter the Great, being superficial and imitative, was the cause of the splitting of the nation into two parts, divided by an almost impassable gulf. The modern culture, penetrating the country in the teeth of the Government, acts in quite an opposite way. Like the fabulous "healing and vivifying water" of our popular legends, it reunites the head of the nation to its maimed trunk, infusing life and soul into the inert social body. It destroys, on the one hand, the artificial barrier between the educated and uneducated classes, between those wearing "German overcoats," and those wearing the workmen's jacket, by destroying the class prejudices inveterate in the latter. On the other hand, in the well-to-do classes, it creates humanitarian and democratic sentiments which draw them toward the masses.

Here lies the real source of the Russian internal struggle. Nihilism, socialism, liberalism, radicalism, are all but off-shoots. The root is European culture. Autocracy and European culture are incompatible. The more Europe advances in her political liberty and culture, the keener will be the disaffection, the jealousy, the shame, and the anger the contrast will produce in Russian minds imbued with it.

This culture, however, is spreading with remarkable rapidity only in towns. In the villages education promised to make as rapid progress as in the towns, owing to the enthusiastic zeal with which the wishes of peasants were met by our educated classes and their representatives. But, as I have explained elsewhere, the government stopped in the most cynical, and I may say unprecedented way this work of enlightenment. And its obstruction, which can be overcome to a great extent in towns, is unfortunately very effective in the villages. I do not want to exaggerate anything; and it would be an exaggeration to say that popular education is making no progress. Some progress is made certainly, even under Count Tolstoi's ministry, but it is extremely slow as compared with the magnitude of the country. Thus culture is as yet the stimulating element of a revolt, and not of a revolution.

But there are circumstances in which a revolt is naturally converted into revolution.

V.

Among the active body of Russian revolutionists voices of bitter complaint are often raised against the want of civil courage, resolution, and faithfulness to their convictions of the bulk of Russian society, which is liberal only in words, shrinking timidly from any manifestation of opinions. The accusation is, it must be confessed, not quite groundless, but this does not prevent it from being unjust at bottom. In great masses the love of freedom can never reach such intensity as to drive them to an attack, the issue of which is an almost inevitable holocaust of the bulk of the assailants. This would be the case only with comparatively small groups of individuals. In all the revolutions the world has ever seen, the masses were set in motion just at the moment when there was a gleam of some chance of victory. The greater these chances the bigger the crowd.

In Russia, where the cultured classes are numerically so feeble, the dangers and difficulties of an open insurrection and the disproportion of forces are so evident, that this " crowd " must naturally be very diffident and slow in entering the lists. Thus the natural difficulties of the struggle, already great, are augmented tenfold. The Russian revolution must for a certain time be the work of a comparatively small group of men, surrounded by a crowd of irresolute sympathisers. They are quite sincere in their sympathy, often willing to give occasional help to the strugglers. But they have no faith in the possibility of success, and cannot, therefore, throw in their lot with the revolution. To inspire this faith in their hearts, and to convert them into actual supporters, the revolutionists must show their strength in deeds and not in words. The great difficulty is to organise a body sufficiently strong to initiate the insurrection and to keep the field for a certain time. If not suppressed the first day, there are great chances that the thousands and thousands who are now irresolute and hopeless would join the banner of the insurrection, rendering it no longer subduable.

There is nothing chimerical in such an expectation in countries brimful of disaffection, and history affords some instances of the success of similar attempts. The temptation to try them is, therefore, very great, I may say irresistible. Neither disappointment nor cruel reprisals can prevent their being renewed again and again. Provided latent discontent exist, there will be always people sufficiently bold and willing to risk their heads again and again for such a golden prize.

The peculiarity in the respective positions of the active and potential revolutionists explains to us another characteristic of this period when the revolution is, so to say, in its incubation. I mean the possibility of preventing it by way of comparatively moderate concessions, the more moderate the earlier they are made. The bulk of society, timorous and worried as it is, prefers to obtain something without struggle and risk to risking everything for more. The extreme party may be satisfied or discontented as it likes, personal feelings and inclinations have little weight in historical evolutions. With good or bad grace they must accept the inevitable. They have no more chance of success, of support, or of continuance.

But in great revolutions, however, there comes a very interesting moment, which is characterised precisely by the reverse—the movement ceases to be manageable. It acquires the character of something fatal, unconscious, incapable of arrest or guidance. The concessions and reforms which the frightened Government, awakening to the danger too late, never fails to make, in order to propitiate the howling monster, are no longer of any avail. They only increase the fermentation, and augment the ardour of the assailants, as so many tokens of the weakness of the enemy. If the leaders of the movement for the time being, frightened by the aspect of what they foolishly think to be the work of their hands, try to arrest it and oppose it, they are pitilessly trampled down by the crowd thronging behind them. New men immediately take the posts they have left vacant, often to repeat the same fallacious experiment, and to fall victims of the same fruitless hesitation. It is no longer in human power to arrest the development of the historical tragedy. The revolution must go on as long as it has not consumed its own fuel. Then, and then only, it remains motionless, like the avalanche which has reached the plain. This indomitable character of the popular moves is one of the most striking features of the great French revolution—the one that frightened most of the good people.

And yet all recognise that it was not always thus in France and Paris. Many times the question was asked, as M. Leroy Beaulieu tells us, when the revolution would be arrested on its path by peaceful reforms. Though he admits that nobody has answered this question satisfactorily, by putting it, all acknowledge, as an incontestable truth, that there *was* such a moment, when concessions, instead of augmenting the fermentation, would have quieted it and prevented the revolution. That, in a word, French society, before entering upon the turbulent revolutionary period, was in a state quite analogous to that through which we think Russia is passing now. And so it was really, but it changed. Was it the intoxication of revolutionary ideas which converted the very modest, timorous *bourgeoisie*, so full of regard for, and obsequiousness to the crown as the *cahiers* of 1789 show them to have been, into fierce, uncompromising leaders and instigators of the proletariat?

There was certainly a good deal of enthusiasm and excitement in this epoch—more than in any other,—just as in modern Russia. But men are always men, and it is quite improbable that the mass of people would under any circumstances become possessed of any very exalted and abstract ideals. If by the magic shoes, described by Anderssen, we could be transported into the epoch of the great revolution at the time of its greatest effervescence, inquiring into the minds and intellectual dispositions and aspirations of every unit composing the collective being—that many-headed crowd, the author of the revolution,—we should find most likely something very incoherent, strange, and contradictory; something resembling the explanatory answers which voters give sometimes when asked to explain private aspirations which induced them to vote as they did. Voices of exalted dreamers and Utopians would sound powerful and passionate. But, on the whole, such spiritual statistics would undoubtedly show a surprising moderation, narrowness of expectation and pettiness of individual desire, especially in the beginning, when the revolution was in its first bloom. So, at least, we may infer from such authentic documents as show the genuine thought of the men of the epoch. There would be, however, one thing not to be found in the public mind, and really distinguishing revolutionary periods from all others; that is, the firm and strong belief rooted in the masses and individuals that the time has arrived when all their grievances are to be set right,—all their desires, the petty one as well as the lofty, to be realised immediately, to-morrow, if not to-day. And since all these desires can never be realised at once, and the realisation of one wish generates a new one, the masses rush forward and forward, always discontented, always turbulent, threatening, ready to be set on fire, certain to be victorious and to carry their point.

I will not enumerate what created in the Parisian crowd such convictions and such desires. These influences were numerous and various, some direct ones, exciting people so as to make them forget the dangers of the struggle; the others, indirect, showing the feebleness of the Government and making people feel that there is little danger in the assault. It is very suggestive, however, to note that even in France, where great development of the town element afforded extraordinary facilities for the direct instigative influences, the most decisive blow to the old *régime* was given by indirect influences, namely, by peasant risings, the revival of the *jacquerie*, the campaign against the castles. M. H. Taine mentions about 300 isolated peasant rebellions during the period. And it is known that the great revolutionary victories, beginning with the famous night of the 4th August, took place after the rising of the peasants.

There was nothing, or very little, of spiritual influence and aspiration in these chaotic peasant risings. Peasants are never influenced by the abstract idea of liberty. Their risings were simply the outburst of despair and misery; the case with all the numerous risings of which the Middle Ages witnessed so many. They had nothing creative in them, and had they occurred at another time they would have been once more drowned in blood without producing any consequence. But they occurred at an epoch when a profound fermentation and striving after liberty was going on in the centres of intellectual and social life. And by materially enfeebling and disorganising the Government, by making a powerful diversion, to use military terminology, the French peasants made the French monarchy an easy prey for the proletariat guided by the *bourgeoisie* of the towns.

Something very similar, though not identical, is approaching in Russia. Peasant insurrections are growing in Russia. In all countries, Russia included, the peasants are a very patient, all-enduring race. They are too much cowed by traditional subjection. They are, moreover, quite isolated. No separate peasant rising has any chance of victory, and no simultaneous rising is possible. They rise out of sheer despair when they cannot bear any more; when their condition is such that they have either to die from hunger and misery, or to take the law into their own hands. Such a moment is approaching for hundreds of thousands, millions of Russian peasants. To give complete evidence of my assertion, I must show what are the momentous economical, intellectual, and moral changes, wrought in our village life since the emancipation of 1861. The modern village and modern peasant are not those of twenty-five years ago. Such a study is too extensive to be made as a parenthesis. Here I will quote only one instance, showing that in some Russian provinces agrarian disturbances are assuming already a somewhat serious character.

At the sitting of June 27th, 1883, the marshals of the nobility of five districts of the Uffa province stated in the name of their electors that the nobility of their respective districts were quite unable to enjoy their landed property. Peasants of Bashkir origin, assisted by peasants of Russian origin, who committed from time to time acts of plunder on their property, have within the last two years declared open war against them. In daylight, in bands armed with axes, clubs, and guns, they come, take possession of the land, and behave as masters. They mow down dozens of acres of grass, and cut down entire forests of wood. At the slightest sign of resistance from the managers, proprietors, servants, or representatives of local authority, the peasants use arms, inflicting severe injuries or death upon their enemies, and they plunder or burn the buildings.

Here are some examples of their proceedings.

On January 13th, 1882, the Bashkir peasants of the village Sharanbush arrived on twenty cars at the estate of M. Tchinghis, drove away the guards of the forest, threatening to kill them, and proceeded to hew a great deal of wood, which was then transported to their village. Two days after— the 15th of the same month,—fifty peasants invaded the same estate and offered violent resistance to the mayor of the district, who tried to prevent them from hewing the wood. In March, April, and May, the incursions became so frequent that it was difficult to ascertain their exact number. One of these invasions was accompanied by the expulsion of the police inspector of the fifth district, together with his men.

On May 5th, 1882, they appropriated and sowed, without M. Tchinghis' permission, a piece of land already ploughed by his men for his own use, and on June 5th they mowed, without the proprietor's leave, several acres of meadow. At the end of the year the incursion turned into regular predatory inroads.

On November 13th the peasants appeared in a band of a hundred men, armed with guns and clubs, and behaved as masters; on the 22nd, meeting with some resistance, they dispersed and disarmed the guards, who owed their life to the protection of the mayor of the district (starshina). In January 1883 the peasants became undisputed masters of all M. Tchinghis' woods, so that the proprietor did not venture to provide himself with wood from his own forest.

In other places things were no better. In December 1881 the Bashkir peasants of the village Abramov invaded in a crowd of seventy to eighty people the estate of Major Tevkeleff, and routed and dispersed the guards and male servants of the farm, though these were supported by volunteers from a neighbouring village. Then they set themselves undisturbed to hewing wood, which they carried safely to their village. Next year these invasions continued. The peasants went with a train of thirty to forty carriages, protected by as many armed men, and behaved as if on their own land. When the chief guard Tchainysheff remonstrated, they threatened to shoot him, and they attempted to kill with their hatchets M. Biglow and his son, who took the part of the proprietor. In February 1883 the peasants, being attacked by the guards, fired a volley against them, and put them to flight.

The nobleman, M. Karvovsky, repeats the same sad dirge :—" From 1882 the noblemen's lands have been lawlessly appropriated by the peasants of Bashkir as well as of Russian origin, assaulting the proprietors and their men, wounding and putting them to death, burning the buildings, and dividing among themselves the arable land thus appropriated."

The nobleman V. Fok confirmed the above statements. Agrarian outrages, according to him, are spreading, and are committed in open daylight, with unheard-of audacity. On his own estate all the arable land is violently appropriated by the peasants, the wood is all hewn down, the guards dispersed, and one of them was brutally killed, then sewn in a sack, and thrown on the road.

Similar events happened in half-a-dozen other places. At the end of 1882, and the beginning of 1883, the agrarian disturbances spread over four districts. The estates of the noblemen Tevkeleffs, Karvovsky, Shafranoff, Goriansky, Pokvistneff, Krotloff, and many others, were appropriated by force. To Mr. Rall, nobleman, the peasants, his former serfs, sent a message intimating to him that they had passed at their meeting a resolution to take for their use one of his fields of about sixty-two acres, and were firmly resolved to carry their resolution into effect. An identical intimation was made to the Colonel of the Body Guards, Tevkeleff. Few proprietors had the audacity to disobey. The peasants never shrank from having recourse to violence. The landlord Karvovsky was beaten almost to death, and saved his life by throwing himself into the river. The manager of General Voronoff's estate, in trying to dissuade from plunder a mob of sixty peasants, was beaten severely, had one rib broken, and died in the hospital. The farms of the noblemen Lode, Aksenoff, Nelken, Beresovsky, were burnt. In the spring of 1883, in Uffa district, the farm of the nobleman Therniovsky was burned, and all the five persons who occupied it massacred. In another the nobleman Zabussoff was wounded by a gunshot.

The landlords, greatly cowed, abandoned by dozens their estates, fleeing to the towns, where the police were better able to protect them, and leaving their estates to their fate.

Such were the facts brought to light at the sitting of June 27th, 1883, of the Uffa nobility. The nobles remonstrated against the laxity of the local authorities, and moved a resolution to petition the Minister of the Interior for measures " intended to re-establish order in the Uffa province and to protect the Uffa nobility against the growing violences of the peasants." The motion was put to the vote by the Marshal of Nobility, and carried by sixty-two votes against eight, the ballot being secret. (*Messenger of Naroduaia Volia, No.* 4, 1885.)

These disturbances among the peasants—chiefly of Bashkir origin—of the four districts of Uffa can be certainly ascribed to a considerable extent to the particularly disgraceful malversation in the land-distribution made by the authorities some ten years ago. But it must be remembered that the whole agrarian arrangement created by the Act of 1861 is in flagrant contradiction to the fundamental conceptions of all Russian peasants as to the tenure of land. It is, therefore, only natural that agrarian outrages and disturbances occur in many other places, assuming sometimes serious proportions. In the spring of 1884, in the province of Don, agrarian disturbances occurred quite similar to those of the Uffa province, and also necessitating the intervention of troops. They were provoked exclusively by the general influences common to all Russian peasants. The landlords, having their estates disposed all around the land of the peasants, and holding in their power roads, pastures, and wells, imposed on the helpless peasants such economic slavery as drove them to ruin and open rebellion. Agrarian crimes began first isolated, then assuming by-and-by the character of inroads. Bands of peasants armed with guns, clubs, and hatchets, plundered farms, driving cattle, stealing corn, burning buildings, and having regular battles and sieges with the proprietors and their men.

The best-informed English papers send now and then reports of the frequency of agrarian crimes throughout Russia—a question on which Russian papers are bound to keep unbroken silence. Quite recently the Odessa correspondent of the *Daily*

News (February 18th, 1886) sent the following interesting account :—

"I am told on the best authority that the number of agrarian crimes is greatly increasing in almost every part of Russia, and especially in the southern provinces. This fact is said to be undoubtedly owing to the incessant agitation carried on in the country by the emissaries of the Revolutionary party (?). A colonel, who is president of one of the many court-martials which are in constant activity in the southern provinces since they have been declared in a state of siege, has given me anything but a satisfactory description of the state of things there. The discontent amongst the peasants is deeper than it ever was before, and the landowners are living in continual fear that the peasants will do them some injury. This statement is not exaggerated. You remember, perhaps, the following words in the recently-published address from the nobility in the Simbirsk district: 'We hope that measures will be taken in order to enable us to live in security on our estates.' The president of the court-martial I have already referred to told me that only about ten per cent. of the offences he had had to judge were of a military nature. All the others were agrarian, Socialist, or Nihilist in their character."

(The reader must remember that all political offences there, which the writer calls Nihilist and Socialist, are dealt with by military tribunals.)

These isolated examples show that all is not peace and obedience in the green fields and hamlets of holy Russia.

Well; from the moment when such disturbances

cease to be isolated, when they spread over provinces as they are spreading now over districts, when they happen in some central province, and not at the extremities of the Empire, some chamberlain of the Tzar, who has a bit of brain in his head, will be able to say to Alexander III., "Sire, it is not a revolt, but a revolution."

The town elements are very feeble in Russia compared with those of the France of Louis XVI. The "diversion" of the agrarian insurgent must be very great indeed to enable St. Petersburg to play the part of Paris. But we have, on the other hand, our compensation in the closer union of the towns with the villages, which disappeared entirely in France at the end of the eighteenth century. The workmen of the towns are many of them peasants who have their family and relatives in the villages, and have kept up their communications with them. The educated classes—the "intelligence" as we call it—are attracted by all their sympathies to the peasants also.

Then another peculiarity of Russia is the enormous amount of combustible elements embodied in men and parties in whom the unheard-of cruelties of the latter day despotism of the Romanoffs have developed an intensity of hatred and resoluteness of action unknown to men under the comparatively mild despotism of the last Bourbons. Any serious symptom of the approaching popular storm will have a tremendous echo in our towns. Surrounded and prompted by the general excitement among the well-to-do and working classes, the subversive elements in which excitement will reach its highest pitch are prepared by their traditions and their utter carelessness about personal dangers, to act with the greatest energy against the central organs of the Government. On the other hand, this excitement will re-echo to the villages. No one who knows our " intelligence " and revolutionist workmen, can doubt that a considerable part of these elements will rush headlong to the villages that rise. The most gifted of them will find means to acclimatise themselves to their new environment, and will give to a Russian *jacquerie* the tenacity, organisation, and military direction, which the French had not. Save the reactionary, Vendéen *jacquerie*, the only one which obtained vast assistance from cultured and intelligent elements, that transformed it from a peasants' rising into regular guerilla warfare, the most dangerous and durable of all. Perhaps the only form of warfare for coping with regular forces after the invention of metallic cartridges and breechloaders, which render in our days open street fighting extremely hazardous. Little Poland, withstanding for fourteen months the efforts of 100,000 Russian bayonets, has shown in comparatively recent times the great tenacity and strength of guerilla warfare, for which Russia in general, with its enormous distances and vast forests and marshes, affords peculiar facilities.

Nobody can force the march of a momentous historical crisis. But it seems but an inference from our social condition to suppose that the crisis will be the combined effort of the town and rural elements. Since the latter have to play a much more active part than in any former revolution, the Russian revolution will very likely assume a more violent and destructive character than any of its predecessors. There is, indeed, much exaggeration on this point. Russian peasants are not at all as wild as they are supposed to be, and their old hatred to all bearing the stamp of civilisation has greatly subsided since the emancipation. But the rural crowd is always more violent when excited than the proletariat of the towns, and it will most likely fulfil some of the gloomy forebodings nourished in respect to it. This cannot be helped.

The conflagration once begun at both ends will cease to be controllable by human will. And it will be the duty of the extreme party, whatever the name it bears then, to take part in the movement whatever it be, to try to minimise its ferocity as far as possible, but to secure its victory at any price, at the expense of any sacrifice.

But is this fierce cataclysm really likely to happen? The Government—a clique of brazen-headed courtiers and sycophants like Tolstoi, Pobedonorzeff, and Katkoff,—*they* are the masters of Russia, not Alexander III. Does it really require for its overthrow the fermentation and violent convulsion of an enormous nation of one hundred millions of people? The classes in which keen discontent is not blinded by ignorance of the cause of their sufferings, will they be really unable to get rid of the absurd and antediluvian autocracy without appealing to the horrors of a popular insurrection? No; we will never admit it for a moment. We believe too much in the patriotism of the Russian people of all classes and shades of opinions—revolutionists and liberals, civilians and military,—to admit for our country the possibility of such a shame. We believe in a political revolution—in a revolt. Through many trials, misfortunes, and fruitless hecatombs of lives the glorious moment of the revival of the Decembrist traditions will come, and it is right that Europe should know beforehand what to expect from it and with whom to side.

THE END.

www.ingramcontent.com/pod-product-compliance
Lightning Source LLC
Chambersburg PA
CBHW031936230426
43672CB00010B/1940